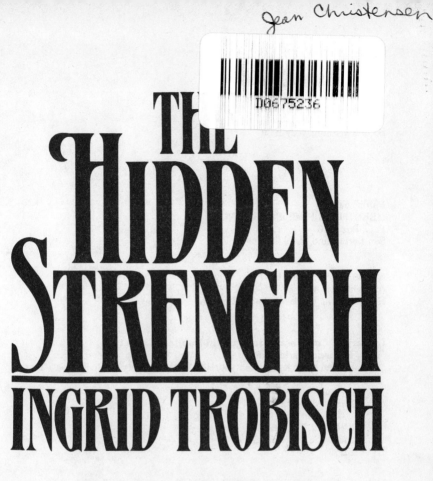

THE HIDDEN STRENGTH

INGRID TROBISCH

*Rooted in the Security
of God's Love*

Jean

in His loving care

Ingrid Trobisch

Here's Life Publishers

First printing, February 1988
Second printing, May 1989

Published by
HERE'S LIFE PUBLISHERS, INC.
P. O. Box 1576
San Bernardino, CA 92402

Library of Congress Cataloging-in-Publication Data
    Trobisch, Ingrid Hult.
    Hidden strength : living your life in the security of God's love / Ingrid
    Trobisch.
    p. cm.
    ISBN 0-89840-200-X
    1. Christian life—1960-   2. God-Love.   I. Title.
    BV4501.2.T72   1988
    248.4—dc 19   87-19284
    CIP

Unless indicated otherwise, Scripture quotations are from *The Holy Bible, New International Version,* © 1973, 1978, 1984 by the International Bible Society, published by Zondervan Bible Publishers, Grand Rapids, Michigan.

Scripture quotations designated KJV are from the King James Version of the Bible.

Scripture quotations designated RSV are from *The Revised Standard Version,* © 1962 by the World Publishing Company, New York, New York.

Scripture quotations designated AMP are from *The Amplified Bible,* © 1975 by Zondervan Bible Publishers, Grand Rapids, Michigan.

For More Information, Write:
L.I.F.E.—P.O. Box A399, Sydney South 2000, Australia
Campus Crusade for Christ—Box 300, Vancouver, B.C. V6C 2X3, Canada
Campus Crusade for Christ—Pearl Assurance House, 4 Temple Row, Birmingham, B2 5HG, England
Lay Institute for Evangelism—P.O. Box 8786, Auckland 3, New Zealand
Campus Crusade for Christ—P.O. Box 240, Colombo Court Post Office, Singapore 9117
A Great Commission Movement of Nigeria—P.O. Box 500, Jos, Plateau State Nigeria, West Africa
Campus Crusade for Christ International—Arrowhead Springs, San Bernardino, CA 92414, U.S.A.

VIRGINIA.
1955

I have just returned from a family reunion at our old home on the Lichtenberg in Austria. My oldest son Daniel, his wife Betty and their three little sons, Michael, Andrew and Peter are now living there. The motto we chose for our reunion, "The love of the family shelters us like a tree," was taken from a poster designed by a twelve-year-old in the American Lutheran Church.

This frontispiece was taken from a sketch I made in one of my journals, after reading a story to my granddaughter Virginia about such a tree. She was five at the time. She sat on my lap and helped me with the sketch – drawing in the leaves and coloring it her way. She even signed it, as you can see.

Contents

Author's Preface

DEDICATION

To my mother
Gertrude Jacobson Hult
whose hidden strength
never ceases
to amaze me

This book is about *Geborgenheit* and how I found it. In my German dictionary, this noun means "a place of safety and security." The verb form, *geborgen sein,* means "to be hidden or sheltered, to be in safety or out of danger."

I named the wonderful old stone house in which I live *Haus der Geborgenheit.* The English equivalent is the "House of Steadfast Shelter." It is a good name, for I am told that the stones used to build the house are millions of years old. I feel safe and secure each time I enter the door of my home. It is a deep symbol for me of being "under the roof" of my heavenly Father's love and of the strength gained from being out of danger because I am there, under that roof.

In the course of the past thirty years I have written three major books. The first one, *On Our Way Rejoicing,*[1] was the story of my parents and the vision which they passed on to their children. This vision took us literally around the globe. The second book was written for men, with the title *The Joy of Being a Woman . . . and What a Man Can Do.*[2] The third, *Learning to Walk Alone,*[3] was about my pilgrimage as a widow.

All three were born out of personal experience. They called to be written. This book, *The Hidden Strength,* also calls to be written. An editor once told me, "You have no excuse to write unless you have something to say which has not been said before." *Geborgenheit,* and how I derived strength from it for life's passages and storms, is the theme of this book. I pray it will direct you to the one who is "our refuge and strength" (Psalm 46:1)

—Ingrid Trobisch

CHAPTER 1

Discovering the Roots

How to identify your true source of strength

Have you ever looked at a friend, a parent or a grandparent and wondered, *What gives that person such enormous strength in times of crisis, conflict or trial? Where does his hidden strength come from?*

I shall never forget my mother's reaction when I called her to tell her of my father's sudden death in Tanzania, Africa. I was a high school senior at Luther Academy in Wahoo, Nebraska, and Mother was in Springfield, Missouri, with my younger brothers and sisters. It was at the peak of World War II — my father had gone back to Africa alone and left his family behind. Now I had to make the hardest call of my young life and break the news of his death to my mother. She answered the phone and greeted me with her usual cheeriness.

"Mother," I said, "I have some bad news for you. Are you strong?"

"Yes, Ingrid," she said slowly. "Tell me what it is."

I read her the cablegram from Dar es Salaam which had been received at our mission office. My father had died on March 18, 1943, from heart failure following malaria.

There was a long moment of silence. Then Mother asked me in a normal, calm voice, "How are you, Ingrid? And how is your grandmother? How is she taking the news of her eldest son's death?"

When I tried to comfort Mother, she said simply, "The future is not dark. The Lord has helped us up until now. He will continue."

Everyone wondered at her strength. Later she told us that on that dark day, my younger brother Carl was sick with the measles and the other children were coming down with them. Out in the chicken coop, she had two hundred baby chicks to care for. She simply had no time to give herself over to grief. I was not surprised. All my life I had watched Mother cope with life's storms and I knew that she had hidden strength.

The Psalm 1 Tree

One of my earliest memories is of my father showing me his small brown leather New Testament in the Swedish language. My grandfather had given it to him in 1906, when my father was eighteen and leaving home for the first time, heading for Luther Academy. Under the inscription and date, my grandfather had written:

The First Psalm

Blessed is the man
   who does not walk in the counsel of the wicked
or stand in the way of sinners
   or sit in the seat of mockers.
But his delight is in the law of the LORD,
   and on his law he meditates day and night.
He is *like a tree* planted by streams of water,
   which yields its fruit in season
and whose leaf does not wither.
(Psalm 1:1-3, italics mine.)

In our little home in the Austrian Alps more than seventy years later, my husband Walter and I had our last quiet time together, and we meditated on this part of that same psalm:

[The righteous man] is *like a tree* planted by streams of water,
> which yields its fruit in season
and whose leaf does not wither.
> Whatever he does prospers (verse 3).

Then Walter wrote these words in his quiet time booklet and shared them with me:

A tree rests.
A tree stands firm.
A tree drinks with its deep roots.
A tree supports, gives Geborgenheit — *shelter, warmth, security.*
A tree bears fruit.
A tree is not in a hurry.
A tree waits for the right time.

Trees and Geborgenheit

To me, trees and their shade have always been a symbol of *Geborgenheit* — a place of safety and security. When I was a child, whenever my world would seem to be falling apart, I would run out of our crowded little stone cottage in the Ozarks, bury my face in the rough bark of "my" oak tree and hug the tree until all was right again. Sometimes I would crawl up in the sheltering branches of my hiding place, a maple, and be "above" the world for a little while.

Trees have many reasons for existence. They were made before man, yet made for man. They are a home for squirrels, insects, birds. Their shade keeps man from getting too hot. They turn carbon dioxide into oxygen. Trees have been called thoughts of God, expressing not only the mind of the creator, but also the magnetic beauty of the instant of creation. One of the first poems I memorized in school was *Trees* by Joyce Kilmer:

> I think that I shall never see
> A poem lovely as a tree.
>
> A tree whose hungry mouth is prest
> Against the earth's sweet flowing breast;
>
> A tree that looks at God all day,
> And lifts her leafy arms to pray;
>
> A tree that may in summer wear
> A nest of robins in her hair;
>
> Upon whose bosom snow has lain;
> Who intimately lives with rain.
>
> Poems are made by fools like me,
> But only God can make a tree.[1]

Deep Roots to Survive Storms

In order to be and do so many different things, a tree needs deep roots. Only when they are deep can the tree grow upward, become strong and withstand storms. I've been told that if a tree is to survive and prosper, the depths of the roots must equal the height of the tree. There must be as much below the ground as there is above it. And those roots need water. The largest trees are those by streams and rivers or in the rain forest areas of the world. When I look at a giant tree I am deeply moved and I pray a prayer I first heard years ago: "O thou Lord of life, send my roots rain."

A tree shows us how to survive storms in our own lives. Deep roots are vital for the health and growth of both trees and human beings, giving the needed stability to survive those storms.

These trees are the ones which also can survive a

fire. One of my friends, who owns a small oak forest in the Ozarks near the Arkansas border, was greatly perturbed when he heard that a forest fire was raging in that vicinity. He mourned the loss of his trees. To his astonishment, when he went to investigate after the fire, he discovered that only the diseased and dead trees had burned. The growing and healthy trees stood unharmed.

A few days later in my father's library I found a book, published in 1885, entitled *Christian Growth*. It described a fire that had swept through one of the vast redwood forests in California, destroying some of the great trees while others, though scorched and blackened, were unhurt. Cutting into the trees, foresters found that those trees which were killed by the fire were already decayed at the heart. The author said, "So the fires of affliction do not destroy true faith — they only test and develop its power." Often ordinary people, confronted with catastrophic circumstances, have been transformed by these circumstances, proving the truth of the German proverb, "What does not kill you, makes you stronger."

Our strength comes from having strong roots. In *Grapes of Wrath,* John Steinbeck describes the agonizing decision of a family faced with leaving their home in the "dust bowl" of Oklahoma to become migrant workers. In a despairing voice Ma says to Pa, "But how can our children know who they are if they don't know where they came from?"

My own roots were sunk into the combined soil of Africa, where I was born; Sweden, the home of all my ancestors; and the Ozarks, where I grew up. Old Moshi, on the slopes of Mt. Kilimanjaro in Tanzania, East Africa, was my birthplace. My parents were pioneer missionaries there. "You were born in one of the most beautiful spots of the earth," my mother told me. My first world journey, together with my parents and two older brothers, began when I was three weeks old. As though in a scene from *Out of Africa,* we traveled down the mountain through the lush coffee plantations of the industrious Chagga tribe, by train to Mombasa, the seaport of East Africa, and from there by ship to Sweden.

When I was four, my father knew that his dream of going back to Africa could not materialize so he took his growing family to the gentle mountains of the Ozarks. It turned out to be a good place for me to grow up. As author Willa Cather has observed, there where a child spends the years between four and fourteen will he find his roots.

My parents' relatives grew up on the black dirt farms of Nebraska and Illinois. When they visited our home in Springfield, Missouri, they examined the earth and found it full of rocks. "What can possibly grow here?" they asked my father.

"Trees and children," he answered quietly.

To commemorate the birth of each of my younger brothers and sisters, my father planted a tree. He also planted one to celebrate his mother's seventieth birthday. These trees and their ever-increasing shade have been a symbol to me of my parents and grandparents. Their roots have strengthened my own roots. "The love of a family shelters like a tree."

When I became an adult and lived for decades in both Africa and Europe, Springfield remained the geographical center of my world. I measured distance by how far away I was from the Queen City of the Ozarks. Now in my "middle adulthood" years, I must be truthful and admit this is where my roots still are. That is, if it is possible for a pilgrim to have roots. Even though the Scriptures do tell us that we are pilgrims, Paul also says that we are "rooted and built up in Him [Christ Jesus], strengthened in the faith" (Colossians 2:7). This is the pilgrim's hidden strength—our *Geborgenheit*. We must be rooted and built up in the person of Christ—safe, secure, nurtured in Jesus as our steadfast shelter.

Tapping Your Hidden Strength

This book can become more personal as you consider the following questions and the others that appear at the end of each chapter. Reflect on them individually or use them as a basis for group study and discussion.

1. Describe a time when you saw someone show incredible hidden strength, or when you have sensed it in yourself.

2. How have you seen ordinary people transformed by catastrophic circumstances? How has a transformation happened to you as you went through a storm or fire in your life?

3. Where are your roots? How can you be a "pilgrim" and at the same time have roots?

CHAPTER 2

Developing Gender Identity

*How to find security
through accepting both
the masculine and feminine in yourself*

A poster in my office depicts a little naked girl standing on the ocean shore, stretching out her arms as if to embrace not only herself but the whole world. The caption underneath says: "To be nobody else."

Recently a young wife told me, "I know that I'm a girl, and although that doesn't always make me happy, I want to accept both the limitations and privileges of it." To know who we are — and to be secure in our identity as men and women — is important. God created us as males and females and I'm sure He had a lot of fun when He did it. "And God saw everything that He had made, and behold it was very good — suitable, pleasant — and He approved it completely" (Genesis 1:31, AMP). God patted Himself on the back when He finished creating the first couple. He desired that *together* they should reflect His image to the world.

True Liberation

By way of contrast, in our day women want to be

"liberated." In the truest sense of the word they should be liberated, but without liberated, redeemed men, there will be no liberated, redeemed women. True liberation cannot be experienced until a woman is able to say honestly and unashamedly, "I love being a woman." Or until a man can say, "I enjoy being a man."

The real issue, I believe, is that men and women are insecure in their fullest gender identity. They feel that if they were to reveal some of their true personality traits—those which are commonly considered as belonging to the opposite sex, or those which are looked down upon by the opposite sex—they would not be accepted. Feeling threatened, they deny or bury those traits. They do not allow themselves to express their true feelings, and therefore they don't know who they really are.

Often a son, unaffirmed in his masculinity by his father, will suffer low self-esteem. Unable to accept himself, he will not know what a true man is. A true man is one who not only recognizes and accepts his masculinity, but has also recognized and allowed his "feminine" traits to develop—traits such as sensitivity, compassion, and a desire to express his feelings. Only when this has taken place will he be able to truly understand a woman. Only then can he become the well-balanced and capable husband, father and leader God has called him to be. (For further insights on this concept, see *All That a Man Can Be,* by Walter Trobisch.[1])

A daughter needs the strength that comes from early affirmation as well. We all know the story of Sleeping Beauty and how she is brought back to life through the kiss of the Prince. This is a wonderful picture of the power that a father has to affirm the beauty and giftedness of the femininity within his daughter.

My father affirmed me. I can never remember him

consciously belittling me. He took me and my coming womanhood seriously.

I was not yet ten when, on a cozy winter Sunday afternoon, he explained to me "the facts of life" while teaching me my Sunday school lesson—the story of Jesus' mother Mary and how she was to have a child even though she had never slept with a man. Father told me I should begin even then to pray for the young man who would someday be my husband. I took my father at his word.

A Symbol of Our Heavenly Father

Because of my relationship with my earthly father, I loved to sit on his lap. It was only a tiny step for me, after his early death, to find a relationship with my heavenly Father and to let myself be totally and unconditionally loved by Him.

In most cases the father is the first man a girl knows. Unconsciously she will think of God in the same way she thinks of her father. If she has had a warm, loving and caring father, it will be much easier for her to have a warm and loving relationship with her heavenly Father. If she has grown up without a father, or with a cold, disapproving father, her image of the heavenly Father will be blurred and distorted. The same is true of her relationship with men in general and, above all, of her marriage relationship.

Living Your Gender

What a difference between men like my father, who was so affirming, and many men described in today's broken world. In order to live our gender, that vital part of the true self and personhood which is created by God, we need role models who are true to that concept, and we need people who will affirm us. Because these are often lacking, we have a great crisis today in gender identity.

Leanne Payne has written several courageous books on this subject, including *The Broken Image* and *Crisis in Masculinity*. She says that for a woman to be whole, not only must her femininity be affirmed, but the masculine within her — self-confidence, independence, strength — must also be recognized, balanced and, where necessary, strengthened. I began to understand what this author meant when a Christian lady doctor counseled me recently, "Ingrid, allow yourself to be strong and creative, to plan and structure, to say just the right word at the right time, to think logically and to show others the way, for that is your calling from God. You have said yes to your femininity. Now learn to say yes to that gentle but strong Daniel in your heart."

Leanne Payne points out that as men have lost the capacity to appropriately touch and call to life (affirm) the feminine within their daughters, the incidence of incest has increased. "Men either affirm positively the masculine and feminine within their sons and daughters, or, by their failure or inability to do so, negate the same."[2]

"When men are healed, the healing of women will naturally follow. It is the father (or father substitute) who affirms sons and daughters in their sexual identity and therefore — because gender identity is a vital part of personhood itself — as persons."[3]

A Christian social scientist, a university faculty member, wrote to me recently after reading the Trobisch books. Her doctoral dissertation exposed patterns in gender-related behavior which do damage to both sexes. She wrote:

> *I have been a Christian for 13 years and am amazed at the lack of solid male Christian presence. In addition, Christian men, as do men historically, have caused women a lot of pain. I have observed this systematically and via convenient samples, and feel that*

there is something very wrong . . . I would like to alert church leaders to the tension and discontent brewing in the church between males and females . . . I have a deep, nagging burden for the church (especially in New York City where I live). Male-female relationships are very strained. If you could hear the anger of the Christian women, it would shock you. I am not an ostrich; I believe conflicts between men and women in the church should be ironed out via prayer, vision and practical measures. But first, there must be admission before there is resolution.

My correspondent then wrote,

Your history, family and life's work are amazing. However, it's the tender love you and your husband shared which impresses me the most. It's very rare, even among Christian couples.

I marveled at what she said about our marriage and thought of the struggles Walter and I had gone through and the emotional energy it had cost us to tend and water that little tree which had been planted on our wedding day. We had watched it grow and bear fruit in spite of ourselves. There had been much pruning, plenty of pain, and a number of crises to work through, and without the hidden strength of being securely rooted in God's love, we couldn't have made it.

Tapping Your Hidden Strength

1. How do you feel about your gender? What kind of affirmation did you receive from your father? From your mother? From others? How did this affect how you feel now?

2. Why are some Christian women angry at men?

3. How can we change this pattern? Does it need changing in your own life? If so, how can you bring about this change?

CHAPTER 3

Learning Single Adulthood

The three-fold secret to hidden strength as a single

To live successfully as a single adult you need confidence.

How many truly confident people do you know?

Is there anything more beautiful than a confident woman?

My grandmother was such a woman of quiet confidence. I'm happy I had a chance to know her well as I went from adolescence to young adulthood, and she became one of my role models.

Confidence comes from and nurtures our hidden strength. "In quietness and in (trusting) confidence shall be your strength" (Isaiah 30:15, AMP). When I was thirteen I had a deep experience of answered prayer which taught me confidence and trust in my heavenly Father.

In my heart I had an intense desire to go to the Luther Academy High School in Wahoo, Nebraska, where my father had attended. It was the school that my grandparents, Swedish immigrants, had helped to build.

Grandmother still lived in the vicinity so I had opportunity to visit the campus. When I told my parents how much I wanted to go to Luther, they sadly told me it would be out of the question because of the expense. It was four hundred miles away from home and, since it was a private school, there also would be tuition to pay. I would have to go to the same country high school near Springfield that my older brothers attended.

Disappointed with their answer, but not ready to give up, I went to my hidden tree every evening after supper. Digging my forehead into the rough bark of the strong oak tree, I closed my eyes and asked my heavenly Father to please keep the promise that I had learned in Mark 11:24: "Whatever you ask for in prayer, believe that you have received it, and it will be yours."

Several weeks went by. No sign of an answer to my prayer. When I wasn't helping my mother in some way, I fixed the hems of my dresses and then packed them carefully with my other treasures in cardboard boxes under my bed.

The first day of school came. Nothing happened. I kept on praying, hoping. The noon mail came. I watched as my father sorted it out. He held up a letter from my uncle, a businessman in Wahoo. Father was smiling as he read: "Would you consider letting Ingrid come and live with her grandmother who should no longer be alone? Ingrid could go to Luther . . . " He even enclosed money to pay for the trip.

My father and I started out that very afternoon in the old family Chevy. He drove through the night, we arrived in Wahoo early the next morning, and I enrolled in school. My tuition was waived, and in my grandmother's cozy little house I had that feeling of "a sheltered place," the *Geborgenheit* I longed for. Most of all I enjoyed the time alone with my grandmother—there were deep bonds between us. I so admired her hidden strength. At the age of forty-three, she had been widowed with eight children, between the ages of two to nineteen, to raise.

Years later I was asked to write a chapter on my life's role model for the book, *Bright Legacy.*[1] I was to tell about the woman who had most influenced my life. I chose my grandmother, Johanna Mathilda, who personified for me the woman described in Proverbs 31:25,26:

> She is clothed with strength and dignity;
> she can laugh at the days to come.
> She speaks with wisdom,
> and faithful instruction is on her tongue.

Grandmother's hidden strength reminded me of Swedish steel, which, it is reported, can stand up under great pressure because of the quality of the ore used to produce it. Grandmother had walked alone but she did so "with strength and dignity." We shared the deep joy of kinship and mutual understanding that comes from being related on both a spiritual and a physical level.

True Education

I finally reached young adulthood, and in learning to cope with it as a single, I was thankful for the peers and teachers I had had at a Christian school. One of them wrote in a Luther College yearbook about the aim of true education:

> Any teacher can fill the waterpots in the class before him, but only the Master can change the water into wine . . . Not until the truth we are teaching has entered the warm, rich stream of the learner's experience can we really say that Christian education has reached the goal. To make life rich and abundant, not only to find the brain and train the intellect, is our aim at this school.

A Chinese proverb says: "If you plant for one year, you plant rice. If you plant for ten years, you plant a tree. If you plant for a hundred years, you educate."

A Threefold Secret

I heard Simone de Beauvoir, a keen French woman author, declare that it is the task of every woman to forget herself and to give herself to others. "But," she asked, "how can she do that if she doesn't know who she is? Some women never learn to know who they are, and that's why they have so little to give others."

Certainly young adulthood is the time to discover who we are and to say yes to being ourselves. Each of us is an original creation of God. In the television program *Upstairs—Downstairs,* I heard Mr. Hudson, the English butler, congratulate Edward, another servant, on a life-changing decision he had made. Hudson said, "That's a part of belonging to yourself. Doing what's right for you to do."

The secret to experiencing this quiet confidence and hidden strength is threefold. We need to know—and to feel—(1) that we *belong,* (2) that we are *worthy,* and (3) that we are *competent.* Only then will we have a true sense of identity, of knowing who we are.

Belonging

We need to *belong.* What a wonderful experience it has been for me, not only to know the love of an earthly family that cares, but also to belong to the family of God.

After my freshman year in college, when I was eighteen, I had a deep experience of faith. My self-righteous religious veneer was broken through. I had come to the end of myself, but the *end* actually became a new beginning. I experienced, like a burst of sunlight, what Paul meant when he wrote to the Corinthians: "Therefore, if anyone is in Christ, he is a new creation; the old has gone, the new has come!" (2 Corinthians 5:17). Now I belonged, really belonged—to the family of God.

Being Worthy

How did it happen? Leaving behind all my efforts at good deeds, I simply asked Jesus to cover me with His robe of righteousness. It was like the parable of the wedding feast which Jesus told His disciples in Matthew 22. Everyone was invited to the wedding feast of the king's son. The requirement was simply that each person put on the wedding garment offered by the ruler of the feast. One guest refused. He thought his elaborate robe far superior to the simple one offered to him. He was thrown out of the banquet hall, exiled.

All through that summer I had been under the conviction of the Holy Spirit, but I had fought against the moment of absolute surrender. I will never forget the walk I took in the deep woods of northern Minnesota where I was attending a youth camp as a counselor. I was tired of the struggle, of trying to prove myself worthy, of "always learning but never able to acknowledge the truth" (2 Timothy 3:7), so I finally just gave up my own tattered robe and exchanged it for His. What a relief! Now I, too, was *worthy,* not because of anything I had done, but because of His righteousness. I could say with the blind man in John 9:25, "One thing I do know. I was blind but now I see."

Being Competent

It was then I learned to know the joy of the Comforter, the Holy Spirit. He is a gentleman, opening the door so that we might see Christ. He never draws attention to Himself. In the Old Testament (2 Chronicles 24:20, RSV) we read that the Holy Spirit "took possession" of the prophet Zechariah in order to pronounce His message. It's as though the Spirit "clothed Himself" with the man. I like that thought, that the Holy Spirit wants to clothe Himself with me, with you. "Do you not know that your body is a temple of the Holy Spirit, who is in you, whom you have received from God?" (1 Corinthians 6:19). I clung to the promise in 2 Timothy 1:7: "For God did not give us a spirit of timidity, but a spirit of power, of love and of self-discipline." The Holy Spirit, who gives us *competence,* is the source of competence. Paul writes to the Corinthians: "Not that we are competent to claim anything for ourselves, but our competence comes from God" (2 Corinthians 3:5).

A Place

On the practical side of single living, I discovered that only the one who has learned to live alone is able to live with another person. I realized that in order to live a fulfilling life as a single, we need two things: (1) We need to have *a place,* and (2) we need to learn to live in harmony with *time.*

Growing up in a large family, I had learned how important it was to have a place. I shared a double bed with a younger sister and had part of a cupboard for my clothes, but I had one cardboard box for my personal treasures. "My" tree also came to be one of my places.

The first gift that God gave to Adam and Eve was a place—the Garden of Eden. When they lost this God-given garden they became fugitives. Later, their son Cain also was obliged to live the life of a fugitive. It was the worst punishment God could give to Cain (who had killed his own brother)—that he would never have a "place."

When I left home for the first time and went to live with my grandmother, I acquired a room of my own and a desk—*a place.* It has been essential in my development as a Christian to have a place for my quiet time. I have noticed in later years, when visiting in homes all over the world, that a wife and mother also needs her place—at least her own desk or table and chair—if she is to be effective. Only then can she truly be a place for others. In our spiritual lives, the lack of a place for a quiet time with God is one of our greatest practical difficulties. Jesus, too, lacked a place in this world: "Foxes have holes and birds of the air have nests, but the Son of Man has no place to lay his head" (Luke 9:58).

My sister, a single missionary, felt that she had no real place when she came home on furlough. Finally, she found a coat that she really loved to wear; it became a symbol for her of God's protecting love. Every time she put it on, she said to herself, *This is my place for now.* She was gripped with sadness when she had to give the coat away before she returned to her station in Africa.

When we suffer because of a lack of a place, we share this with our Lord. The only two places the world had to offer Him were the manger and the cross.

Making Order Can Create a Place

In the deeply-felt prayer letter that Walter wrote to our friends shortly before his death, he spoke about the importance of having a place:

> *This is the challenge of the hour, to make room by making order. Maybe we should begin by straightening up the things we can see—our drawers, shelves, closet, and also our finances. But above all, we must make order inwardly.*
>
> *To make order creates new space, but we also need space in which to make order. In a small room where things are heaped up one on top of the other so that we cannot even turn around, we cannot make order. To turn to God takes room as well. Our greatest danger is that we might lose this room needed to turn around and to repent . . . The servant at the wedding feast reports "and there is still room" (Luke 14:22, KJV) at God's great banquet*

table to which all of us are invited. To Moses, who longed to see God's glory, the Lord said, "Behold, there is a place by me" (Exodus 33:21, KJV). Then God put Moses in the cleft of the rock and covered him with His hand.

The cleft is the place of grace. Hemmed in by the narrow walls of rock—here is God's place for us in this world.²

How I Found My Place

It was after my summer youth camp experience in Minnesota that I came to the deep assurance that I was safe in God's tent, that I had a dwelling-place in His steadfast love. I hung on to the promises of Isaiah 43:1 and 4: "Fear not [Ingrid], for I have redeemed you; I have called you by name, [Ingrid,] you are mine . . . Since you are precious and honored in my sight, and because I love you." In my Bible I underlined and claimed the promise of Isaiah 45:2,3:

> I will go before you
>   and will level the mountains;
> I will break down gates of bronze
>   and cut through bars of iron.
> I will give you the treasures of darkness,
>   riches stored in secret places,
> so that you may know that I am the LORD,
>   the God of Israel, who calls you by name.

Living With Time

My son David teaches at a university and observes many singles as well as young marrieds. Recently I asked him, "What's the secret of success among the young people you know?"

His answer was swift. "The ones who succeed eat regularly, sleep regularly and clean house regularly." He admitted that for him and his wife, the latter was sometimes the most difficult.

As a senior at Augustana College in Rock Island, Illinois, I failed a 19th century philosophy test because I didn't find time to study for it properly. When I reported to the dean of women, I poured out my sob story: a heavy academic load plus two part-time jobs. She didn't fall for it, but looked me straight in the eye and said, "Are you sure you're not giving in to self-pity? Go and do better next time. Plan your work—and work your plan."

The concept of time troubled C. S. Lewis, too. He once said, "We are not actually made for time. A fish lives in the water and isn't troubled by the water, but we live in time and are constantly troubled by it. Therefore we were not made for time. We were made for eternity. We are timeless creatures."

And yet, like C. S. Lewis, we must live, redeeming the time. We dare not waste time, kill time, or even spend time. We must *invest time.* I find it helpful to think of time as a bank account, received at birth. There are no deposits, only withdrawals. No man can add to his stature or to his days.

A child waits for time—he waits for things to happen. He even feels controlled and pushed by time, while an adult sees time as a wealth which he can invest. An adult does not wait passively for things to happen, but has a plan and knows that God often gives him the responsibility to "make things happen." I find that the Holy Spirit gives me nudges: "Write that letter today." "Call your brother, your friend." I hear these nudges once, sometimes twice, and if I am not obedient the third time, I know that I have missed God's best timing and that I will miss a blessing and perhaps His kingdom will be impoverished.

The present moment is the only time we have. Often the worst decision we can make is indecision. Not making any decision about the use of time allows external forces to make our decisions for us.

General Ulysses S. Grant once had to make a tough decision during an important battle. "Are you sure your decision is right?" one of his subordinates asked him.

"No, I'm not sure," he answered. "The only thing I am afraid of is indecision."

When Alexander the Great was asked about his secret as to how he would conquer the world, his simple answer was: "By not delaying."

I have a little motto on my desk, which has been a constant challenge to me: "Do it now."

Eleanor Roosevelt, certainly one of the most remarkable women of our century, was asked what her secret was about time. She answered: "If I have something to do, I just do it."

At one point while I was a young single Christian, time took on a particular significance for me. I realized it was my time for decision—my time to find God's will for my life. In college I had learned to defend what I believed, to witness to my faith and to give an answer to those who asked me. But now I knew that God had something further for me and I became aware that He was calling me to be a missionary. I also knew, however, that crossing the ocean did not automatically make me a missionary. I knew I would have to make a firm commitment, so that God's plan, purpose and program for my life could be realized. As a single adult, that is how I would find my hidden strength.

Tapping Your Hidden Strength

1. What was your first experience of answered prayer?

2. Can you name people who have a quiet confidence about them?

3. Do you have a sense of belonging, of being worthy, of competence? How did you acquire these feelings?

4. Where is your "place"? Can you find – or make – it?

5. What is your relationship to time? Do you know how to enjoy the sacrament of the present moment? Have you learned this secret:

>   Decide what's important. Do it.
>   Decide what's not important. Don't do it.

6. Do you have a daily quiet time in order to plan your time?

CHAPTER 4

Living Your Commitment

Your opportunity to record it and make it authentic

One day when I was ten, my parents asked me to watch Gus, my two-year-old brother, while they went for a walk together. I accepted the responsibility. Everything went fine until I remembered the book hiding under my pillow. Moments later, with my back up against a tree trunk in our yard, I buried my head in the book and forgot my commitment. Suddenly there was a loud cry. Gus had fallen from his red wagon and cut his lip badly on a rock. I don't remember being punished for my negligence, but I do remember my father saying, "Gus will always have a scar because of his fall. When you see it, you will be reminded that you didn't do as you promised."

Today when I look at my good brother, now in his fifties, I still see that faint scar, and it always reminds me to take my commitments seriously.

Commitment—What Is It?

One pastor described commitment as "a pledging, a binding of oneself to a person, a cause, or a truth—regardless of future cost."

My brother-in-law, Vincent Will, also has a definition for commitment. "It is," he says, "the first step in entering the new life. A lack of commitment is simply short-term faith, something that is returnable. When you make a commitment to God, you are giving yourself to someone who is greater than you are, who is the Way, the Truth and the Life. It's the last movement you make before God takes over. You commit yourself to God's beauty parlor and give yourself over to the object of your faith."

First comes faith, the basis of our relationship with our Lover, Jesus Christ — and then comes the commitment to Him and His plan for us, our works. Commitment is never forced. It is given freely.

My Own Commitments

As I look back over some of my own commitments, I remember my public confession of faith when I was thirteen — that I believed in God the Father, the Son and the Holy Spirit, and that I renounced the forces of evil, the devil and all his empty promises. In order to seal this commitment, the pastor laid both hands on my head and prayed the following prayer:

Father in heaven, for Jesus' sake, stir up in Ingrid the gift of your Holy Spirit, confirm her faith, guide her life, empower her in her serving, give her patience in suffering, and bring her to everlasting faith.

Three years later, when we received the news of my father's death in Africa, I stood up before our student body and declared:

It's hard to understand why my father should be taken now when he's so badly needed in Tanzania. My sisters and I are now more determined than ever to give our lives entirely to the expansion of God's kingdom here on earth, in the manner and place which to Him seems best.

I had made another commitment — but it scared me,

because I had no idea how I could fulfill it. God takes us seriously, though, when we reach out to Him and lay our lives at His feet.

On July 10, 1944, after finishing Luther Academy, I had a chance to nail down that commitment at a Bible camp in northern Minnesota. Those of us who attended were invited to make a written commitment and sign it in the presence of three of the leaders.

I signed it, Ingrid J. Hult, and dated it. Underneath my name are the signatures of the three men of God who witnessed my commitment: Paul J. Lindell, Clifford Michelsen and Evald J. Conrad, whose combined ministries have reached around the globe.

I pasted that sheet in the middle pages of my Bible between the Old and New Testaments. It is still there, worn now, but like my brother's scar, it still reminds me.

You will find a complete copy of the content of that document at the end of this chapter in case you would like at this time to make a similar commitment to your Lord. Read it carefully and prayerfully, sign it, date it, and have it witnessed if you can. It will mean a great deal to you in years to come. It can clarify your purpose in life, and it may prove to be a source of hidden strength for which you will always be grateful.

Another three years would pass before I made my public commitment. By then I had graduated from Augustana College, taken the mission course at the Lutheran Bible Institute in Minneapolis, and been accepted as a missionary with the Sudan Mission. The day came when I was commissioned to go to Cameroun, West Africa. It was a solemn moment as the leaders of the mission and pastors of the district laid their hands on my head and blessed me for this task.

I didn't know that a young German exchange student was standing in the back of the crowded church, and that he heard a quiet voice telling him, "This young woman whom you see kneeling at the altar will someday be your wife." He shrugged it off as completely unreal.

A few days later I left for France where I was to spend long months in language study before sailing on to Africa.

I kept my commitment. There was nothing very romantic about it. Taking one day at a time, I completed that block of study and got my teaching certificate in preparation for work in French-speaking Cameroun. After a year and a half, I had achieved my goal and was ready to leave for my mission post. In the meantime I had become better acquainted with the young German student, who was now a pastor in Ludwigshafen, but we were not ready for a commitment. "A Christian is one who can wait," our pastor told us.

Commitment in Marriage

We waited, and eventually the time was right for us to enter into the commitment of marriage.

According to Dr. Theo Bovet, a renowned Swiss physician and marriage counselor who was also a colleague of Paul Tournier, relationship is the basis of commitment. Often he tells young couples: "First you choose the one you love, and then you love the one you have chosen."

In an article entitled "Did I Marry the Wrong Person?" Dave Veerman says:

> The bottom line for successful marriage is commitment. I believe that any two people, committed to God and to each other, can be happy together. But conversely, any two people, no matter how compatible and well-suited to each other they may be, can be miserable together. Commitment makes the difference.

Don't fall for the lie that the grass is greener elsewhere. Don't let yourself think that your present marriage is a big mistake, and that somewhere else there is someone who is perfect for you. God has a great plan for you and your spouse, but He must be the center of it. Commit yourselves to Him and to each other.[1]

Commitment to Projects

How well I remember a cold evening years later, in February 1963, when I walked briskly through the streets of New York with a great new joy in my heart. I had worked on a writing project for ten years in Africa besides being a busy wife and mother. I had done the necessary research, had succeeded in getting a publisher interested in the story, and had been given a contract for the book, still in outline form. I studied the small print on the official blue document. Several days later I signed the contract, thereby making yet another commitment. I was to deliver the first draft of the manuscript for *On Our Way Rejoicing* by September first of that year.

As I took that first step, little did I know how long the road ahead of me would be. Nor did I dream of the doors it would open for our future writing ministry. That commitment nailed down the call I had felt for many years to write the story of what happens when a whole family says, "Here am I, Lord. Send me!" as Isaiah did in chapter 6, verse 8. I was often ready to give up, but I hung on to the promise of Psalm 118:17: "I will not die but live, and will proclaim what the LORD has done."

No Looking Back

All the things I learned then have helped me in subsequent commitments. Jesus didn't mince words when He said to those who would follow Him, "No one who puts his hand to the plow and looks back is fit for service in the kingdom of God" (Luke 9:62). This "looking back" can be either a resting on your laurels or a sinking in your past failures. In order to plow a straight furrow you have to keep your eyes on the goal. One of the old Swedish hymns which my parents sang together was "I Look Not Back." The Swedish revivalist Oskar Ahnfelt wrote the music and Annie Johnson Flint wrote these words:

I look not back; God knows the fruitless efforts,
    The wasted hours, the sinning, the regrets.
I leave them all with Him who blots the record,
    And graciously forgives, and then forgets.

The last verse was my favorite:

But I look up—into the face of Jesus,
    For there my heart can rest, my fears are stilled;
And there is joy, and love, and light for darkness,
    And perfect peace, and every hope fulfilled.

Our Greatest Commitment

To commit ourselves to Him means that not even those whom we love most on a human level—our own family—should come between God and us.

How could my father leave his wife and children to go back across the ocean at a time of great danger? There was a great need in the mission fields of East Africa and he was asked to return. Inwardly, he was tormented for he knew that if he said yes, it would mean separation from his wife as well as his growing children who needed a father. If any man loved his family, my father did. And yet his call to serve in Africa was clear.

On the trip from New York to Capetown his ship was torpedoed and sunk in the mid-Atlantic by a German warship. Miraculously, he and his fellow passengers were saved. When he arrived back in the United States, his friends and relatives said, "Surely you will stay home now at this time of danger."

But a year later he got passage again — this time on a cargo ship filled with explosives. He sent us a cablegram when he arrived safely in Capetown.

A few months later he made the supreme commitment of his own life, and was buried in a sandy grave in Dar es Salaam.

> If anyone comes to me and does not hate his father and mother, his wife and children, his brothers and sisters — yes, even his own life — he cannot be my disciple (Luke 14:26).

Commitment of Love

The church in Ephesus was a very successful church. They worked hard, endured hardships and fought against heresy, but something was dreadfully wrong. They had forgotten the most important part of commitment, their first love. They needed to fall in love again with their Savior. Jesus' message to them was clear: "Yet I hold this against you: You have forsaken your first love" (Revelation 2:4).

Someone has said, "God respects us when we work for Him, but He loves us when we sing." He's not looking for a paid housekeeper, but for a bride. Commitment means that I entrust my heart and life to Him, and respond to His love, as a bride responds to her bridegroom.

Tapping Your Hidden Strength

1. What commitments have you made in your life?

2. What hinders you from making a commitment?

3. What do you feel about Dr. Bovet's statement, that first we choose the one we love and then love the one we have chosen? Is it valid for today's world?

4. How is the "first love" of Revelation 2:4 expressed in your life?

PERSONAL COMMITMENT DOCUMENT

THIS I BELIEVE:

1. I believe that God created this world and all that is in it for His glory; that He has created me and has given to me all that I possess; that because of this, and also because He has redeemed me with His own precious blood, I belong completely to Him. Romans 11:36; Psalm 24:1; 1 Corinthians 6:19,20; Revelation 4:11, 5:9,10; Colossians 1:16; Acts 17:23-31.

2. That God calls me to recognize and to delight in His ownership of me and all that I have; that He asks me to yield myself whole-heartedly and unreservedly to do His will; that He desires and directs me to always live as in His presence and conduct all my affairs as a faithful steward and caretaker of His possessions. Proverbs 23:26; Colossians 3:23; 1 Corinthians 9:16,17.

3. That God has a definite purpose, plan and program for my life. The days which were ordained for me were recorded in God's book even before I was born. But only as I yield and surrender my all to God and His will and purpose can His plan for me be attained. On the other hand, in the measure I live for self, price, and pleasure, will my life be a waste and God's purpose for me made void. Psalm 139:14-18; Isaiah 49:1; Ephesians 2:10; Galatians 1:15,16; Jeremiah 1:5.

4. That when I thus yield to Him, He gladly receives and takes full possession of my life; that He will then conform me day by day to His will, that all things and circumstances will work together for good and contribute to fulfill His purpose for me; that He will empower me by His Holy Spirit and lead me into joyous, victorious, purposeful and fruitful life. Romans 12:1-4; John 6:37, 15:16; Romans 8:28; 2 Corinthians 2:14.

5. That it is pleasing to the Lord and also help-ful to my faith to openly and definitely declare before others my surrender and dedication to God; that in seek-ing the will and purpose of God for my life it is right and according to the plan of God for me to commit myself also to the fellowship of God's people and to those who have been placed over me in the Lord; that as I willingly sub-mit myself to the Holy Spirit through this fellowship, He will teach, train, and prepare me and finally lead me to the calling and commission which He has for my life. 2 Corinthians 8:5; Hebrews 13:7,17,24; Acts 13:1-4.

MY COMMITTAL:

Believing all this with my whole heart, O my God, I now present myself to Thee, by Thy tender mercies alone, and ask Thee to make me entirely Thine. I mean this to include everything that I am and have — body, mind, and soul; my gifts and abilities; my time and fu-ture; my home, goods and money; my family and loved ones; my position and ambitions; my likes and dislikes; my habits and ideas; and all other things that I by nature have counted as my own.

I lay all this on Thy altar and reckon it all, from this moment on, to be Thine alone. And now I believe that according to Thy promise Thou dost take me, and that Thou wilt continually cleanse me from all sin and shame, and work in me both to will and to do Thy good pleasure.

Furthermore, I also gladly commit myself to the leadership of the Holy Spirit in and through the fellow-ship of God's people, to those who have been placed over me in the Lord, and those who with me are seeking to give their utmost for God's highest purpose. I hereby join together with them in seeking to know and to follow the will of Christ, and I am now ready to obey whatever leading the Holy Spirit may give through this fellowship.

So now I commit my way unto Thee, O Lord, and I will trust Thee to bring it to pass in Thine own way. "I know whom I have believed, and am persuaded that He is able to guard that which I have committed unto Thee against that day."

Signed _____

Date _____

"First they gave their own selves to the Lord,
and to us through the will of God" (2 Corinthians 8:5).

Witnesses:

_____

_____

_____

CHAPTER 5

Experiencing: Stress Distress Unstress

Six steps to unstress

As I write this, I am under stress. I am behind schedule, and many different projects are demanding my time and attention. I am guilty of procrastination, putting off until later what should be done now. I tend to forget that my proper use of time involves staying in the "now now" while planning for "future nows." Maybe stress comes when *we* are trying to do God's work, as my brother just suggested.

We can define stress as any life situation that consistently bothers us and causes us to be upset. I like the picture of the violin string. If it is too taut, it snaps. If too slack, it will not make music.

Recently I was living in my daughter's home because she thought I had been working too hard and she wanted me to rest. She tried to remove all sources of outside stress—and she succeeded to the point that I became so lazy I could barely write a postcard. A Christian nurse later explained to me that we really need stress in order to keep us going, to make the music. Stress is dangerous only when it becomes a lifestyle of dis-stress. But, if we look around, we can find a number of things that will relieve stress for us.

Stress Relievers

I read somewhere that we need fifteen *hearty laughs* a day. Perhaps there is no greater stress-reliever than a hearty laugh. No society has suffered persecution throughout the centuries like the Jewish people, yet their sense of humor is fine-tuned and famous for relieving tense situations. They exemplify the Scripture: "A merry heart doeth good like a medicine" (Proverbs 17:22). Laughter is the therapy, the "internal jogging," that relaxes all those muscles inside us that have become tense with the pressures of life.

I remember the "laid-back" missionary who was responsible for providing electricity and water for three hundred students and twenty-five faculty members on the campus of Cameroun Christian College. The power was provided by generators which malfunctioned a good part of the time. When we told him that we had neither light nor water in our little home, he just laughed and reassured us, "If you think it's bad today, just wait until tomorrow."

Another stress reliever is an *attitude of thanksgiving.* One day when I was perturbed about my unfinished "to-do" list, a good friend gently reminded me, "Ingrid, why aren't you thankful for all the things that you have done? Satan, the great accuser, wants to take away your peace by bringing to your mind what you have not done. The Holy Spirit is the great encourager and comforter. Why should you be harder on yourself than He is? Why not take your list and ask Him to show you all the things you do *not* have to do today? And thank Him for that." I did it, and it certainly helped.

The next reliever of stress we could think about is a *proper perspective on priorities*. Perhaps you recognize this line from an old hymn:

> Each victory will help you
> some other to win.

Every small step forward helps. "Take the next indicated step," my accountant brother told me one day when I was overwhelmed. I sat quietly and sorted out my priorities, and the next step became clear.

I've always loved the psalmist's repeated declaration: "The LORD is my High Tower." When you go up in a high tower you can get the right perspective on things and see that which is small as small and that which is big as big.

In *Women Under Stress*, Randy and Nanci Alcorn say: "Adapt to what you cannot control, control and influence what you can, and leave the rest to Him. And remember when you do, it will be in bigger, better and stronger hands than yours."[1]

When I am quiet and listen to His voice instead of running to and fro, I am amazed at what can happen. According to John 10:4, His own sheep know His voice. The more sensitive we are to our gentle Shepherd's instructions, the more effective will be our use of time. He does not send us on a wild goose chase.

Besides all of the planned time for those threatening lists of things to do, we need to allow for unplanned time, giving room to spontaneity and impulsivity. Once in a while we need to be able to say, "I have nothing to do," and then release our stress and recuperate through relaxation. Why not dream a little, too? Our mental health requires that we not be unduly restricted by time.

Over and above our have-to-do lists, we need to develop several "choose-to-do's"—fun things to use our time for. To me this means carrying a little sketch pad so I can draw a vase, a candlestick, a flower or a tree when it's appropriate. I occasionally need to let go of my orderly left brain that wants to give everything meaning and purpose and let the creative right brain have a chance.

God's Time

God has given me enough time to do what He wants me to do. Am I trying to cram too much into a day? Isn't it wonderful that after God created the world—He could have done it in one day, but He took six—He then rested? It's a great discovery to know that God is not in a hurry, and we find in Isaiah 28:16 (KJV) that He gives us that same freedom: "He that believeth shall not make haste." We can learn from our peaceful God to live one day at a time. "Do not worry about tomorrow, for tomorrow will worry about itself. Each day has enough trouble of its own" (Matthew 6:34). Let's just relax and do what He wants us to do today.

Our Power Source

How do we know what He wants us to do today? Every morning when I wake up I plug in my little hot-pot and make that cup of tea which seems to help get me going. I pray as I do it, "Lord, help me to plug into your power source." Only when there is that inner connection, can I hear His voice and receive through His Holy Spirit the directions for my day.

We read in Mark 1:35 that Jesus had His quiet time. "Very early in the morning, while it was still dark, Jesus got up, left the house and went off to a solitary place, where he prayed."

His disciples came out to look for Him and when

they found Him, they exclaimed: "Everyone is looking for you!"

Jesus replied, "Let us go somewhere else — to the nearby villages — so I can preach there also. That is why I have come" (Mark 1:38). His directions were clear. A day without a quiet time is like a boat without a rudder. Instead of setting a straight course, we allow ourselves to be danced around by whirling wind and waves.

In his little booklet, "Martin Luther's Quiet Time," Walter wrote:

> For Luther, praying does not mean just talking. It also means being silent and listening. To him prayer is not a one-way road. It works both ways. Not only is he talking to God, but God is talking to him — and the latter is the most important part of prayer. Bible study is prayer . . . Many Christians are enriched in their quiet time by asking themselves these four questions about a text:
>
> 1. What am I grateful for? (Thanksgiving)
>
> 2. What do I regret? (Confession)
>
> 3. What should I ask for? (Prayer concerns)
>
> 4. What shall I do? (Action)
>
> Luther writes to his barber: "If the Holy Spirit should come when these thoughts are in your mind, and begin to preach to your heart, giving you rich and enlightened thoughts, then give Him the honor, let your preconceived ideas go, be quiet and listen to Him who can talk better than you; and note what He proclaims and *write it down,* so will you experience miracles as David says: 'Open thou mine eyes that I may behold wondrous things out of thy law' [Psalm 119:18, KJV]" . . .

The writing down, as Luther suggests, is a form of the incarnation of God's Word. It becomes tangible, visible and concrete. It forces us to be precise, definite and particular. Monotony is replaced by variety and surprise. Taking notes enables us also to check whether we have carried out what we planned in the morning. A Chinese proverb says, "The palest ink is stronger than the strongest memory."

Writing down what God has told us is also a great help in sharing when meeting with our prayer partner — also for decision-making in marriage. My wife and I agree on the same text for daily Bible study. This is especially helpful in periods when we are separated. When we meet again we can read to each other what we have written down in our quiet times and experience "wondrous things."[2]

That practice helped relieve stress for both of us.

Shouldering Our Stress

My grandmother used to say that when God gives us a burden He lays it on shoulders strong enough to bear it. "God is our structural engineer," Randy and Nanci Alcorn write. "He knows our needs, He knows our load bearing capacity, our limits. He allows us to live under stress, yes, but never lays upon us a load greater than what He made us [able] to bear."[3]

Give me strength
to rest without guilt,
to run without frenzy,
to soar like an eagle
Over the broad breathless canyons of the life
you still have for me both here and beyond.[4]

Stress and Disease

From the research which the Alcorns did for their chapter about stress and disease they wrote:

Harmful, invisible processes take place under stress, including the production of excessive lipids (fat) in the blood. Long-term stress tears down the walls of the arteries. The body responds by laying down cholesterol plaques to repair the damage. If the stress continues long enough, the cholesterol continues to build up and the arteries become more and more narrow and hardened. This restricts the blood flow and therefore demands higher blood pressure in order to get blood to the extremities. This in turn creates more pressure against the arterial walls, resulting in more damage and still more excessive production of cholesterol.

Many people know the dangers of high cholesterol and attempt to control it by eating less red meat and eggs. That's good. But a single outburst of anger throws us into overdrive and can produce in our bodies the cholesterol equivalent of a dozen eggs![5]

Stressful/Restful

I like the word *rest*. *Restful* instead of *stressful*. The same letters are in both words; they're just rearranged. Matthew 11:28,29 uses the word *rest* two times: "Come to me, all you who are weary and burdened, and I will give you rest. Take my yoke upon you and learn from me, for I am gentle and humble in heart, and you will find rest for your souls." One of my favorite verses in the Old Testament is Exodus 33:14 where the Lord says to Moses, "My presence will go with you, and I will give you rest." Another translation says, "I will set your mind at rest."

In *Making Sunday Special,* Karen Mains reminds us of our need for rest:

God gives us fifty-two Sabbaths, or seven and a half weeks, of vacation time each year—time during which we are to do no work. As Thomas Aquinas put it, each week one goes on a day of vacation with God. This helps us "to rediscover places inside ourselves that can get rusty without use."[6]

In a magazine article, Karen also writes:

Sabbath rest is like a good sleep after insomnia

. . . I am often amazed by just how completely relaxed I become through Sunday observance when in the afternoon I honor the family tradition by napping. These Sunday afternoon naps are usually a deep sleep, a sign that I have allowed the creative initiative so integral to my personality to become still . . . It is like waking and thinking gratefully, *Oh, I have slept well.*[7]

Steps to Unstress

When I asked my first editor, Ed Sammis, affectionately known in our family as Uncle Sam, how he coped when he had a mountain of work ahead of him, he replied, "First, I lie down and take a nap, and then I tackle the mountain."

I have followed his advice often. But how do you get started? These steps have helped me in tackling my mountain and watching stress/distress become unstress:

1. Get things in order.

2. Have a cup of hot tea.

3. Do the least desirable task first. I learned that from my very effective mother-in-law. She also encouraged me to understand and accept that nothing in life is 100 percent perfect. We must be satisfied with the imperfect.

4. Divide and conquer. I call this the Swiss cheese method — making little holes in a big project. Or like my friend Jean says, "The way to eat an elephant is one bite at a time."

5. Cut off escape routes. I did this today when I loaned my car to someone so I wouldn't be tempted to leave my desk.

6. Give yourself a reward for finishing the task or a phase

of the task. I'm going right down to Swenson's for a milk shake now that this chapter is finished.

Tapping Your Hidden Strength

1. Identify the three biggest stressors in your life right now. Why are they stressful?

2. What happens to you physically when you are under stress? Emotionally? Mentally and spiritually? In your close relationships?

3. From this chapter, select three suggestions that appeal to you for handling stress. Describe how each suggestion will help you the next time you are under stress.

CHAPTER 6

Being Married

Six ways to test and prove your love

The only thing more difficult than living alone is living with another person. And that is why only the one who has learned to live alone is ready to get married. I believe the reason so many marriages are sick today is that no man can answer all his wife's felt needs, and no woman can meet all her husband's needs. In fact, each may create even greater needs in the other. Only one true Lover, Jesus Christ, is able to satisfy completely the innermost desires of a person's heart.

It was my privilege to know Dr. Theo Bovet, the Swiss physician quoted in chapter 4. A tall man, when he stood up to give a message on the secrets of marriage, waves of expectation swept his audience. He began: "If you want to suffer shipwreck, and I mean real shipwreck, where you've lost all your baggage and are floating around in the water with only a life-jacket to keep you from drowning, then just get married."

Marriage a Journey

I finally understood what he was saying when I got

married. As a romantic young woman growing up in the post World War II period, I thought of marriage as something you achieved when you stood at the altar and said, "I do." It's the same idea that many people have about becoming a missionary. Neither a marriage nor an effective missionary service is achieved in this way.

Today I tell young couples on their wedding day: You will need to work on your marriage. It is not a completed product that will be dropped into your lap. You will learn as I did that you will have to rid yourself of illusions. After three decades of marriage, I realized that Walter and I had worked hard on it every step of the way. Marriage is not something which can be improvised. You are both embarking on a long voyage, untrained, in a frail little boat headed, inevitably, for stormy waters. The Germans put it clearly when they say: "A man (or woman) must train for every profession, except for the most difficult — that of being married." There may be some days when you are safely anchored in the harbor, but that's not what boats are built for. They are built for sea travel.

Walter and I had a few safe harbor days, but most of the time it seemed we were out on the ocean, bailing water, pulling people from the sea and into the boat, and trying to keep our own signals straight as husband and wife. During all those times we needed our strong co-pilot, the Holy Spirit of God. And we needed the encouragement of fellow Christians who would cheer us on from their own boats nearby. We always made it a point to belong to some church or fellowship group where our brothers and sisters in Christ could correct us and support us.

Romantic love will not support you. It can only last from three months to three years, according to Robert Johnson in *We: Understanding the Psychology of Romantic Love.*[1]

When I say romantic love, I mean falling in love with a dream image, often seeing the loved one as a projection of ourselves, instead of the real person he or she is. It is our preconceived concept of the emotion called love that gives us pleasure and joy in the anticipated presence of another, and therefore the emotion tends to be superficial. What we need is that "stirring the oatmeal" kind of love, as Dr. Johnson describes it. Love is a decision, a judgment. It involves the intellect and the will. True love means that the security and well-being of your partner are as significant to you as your own. We read in Ephesians 5:28 that "a man shall love his wife as his own body."

I am reminded again of Dr. Bovet's statement: "First you choose the one you love and then you love the one you have chosen." It is as simple and as profound as that. When my oldest daughter got married, her husband told us that before he had proposed to her he had gone to a quiet and isolated place for two weeks in order to ask for God's guidance in his choice of his future wife. He didn't know if she would say yes or not, but he came back with the assurance that he should ask Katrine to be his wife. She accepted immediately.

At my youngest daughter's wedding in Austria, during the family festivities the groom's parents presented the young couple with a chest of silverware. Each piece was engraved with the initials *E* and *R* for Ernst and Ruth. Ernst's father said to the young couple, "Remember, this is for life!" Their choice was to be permanent.

Marriage a Calling

Outside of our relationship with our Lord, the choosing of a life partner is certainly the most important and life-changing decision we make. I believe marriage should be a "calling." When we have this sense of guidance and of being called together, we can experience in a greater measure the precious gifts that God wants to give us in our marriage.

I shall never forget that day I knew beyond a doubt that God had called me to be the wife of Walter Trobisch. I was in the savannas of West Africa, walking down a lonely road leading to our bush station at Poli, Cameroun. Walter and I had met briefly at Augustana Seminary in Illinois where he was an exchange student from Germany. I had not been overly impressed by his personal appearance then, for he did not correspond to my romantic dream of how my future husband should look. (Nor did I for him!) Then I left for France and my language studies before going to Cameroun. During that time Walter and I had a chance to correspond and get better acquainted. When he came back to Germany he invited me to visit him. Then we said goodbye at the railroad station in Heidelberg and I boarded the train, returned to France, and went to my ship in Bordeaux for Douala, Cameroun. The only clear guidance we had as we separated were the words of our pastor: "A Christian is one who can wait."

While Walter pastored a large congregation in Ludwigshafen, Germany, I taught French classes, helped with the sick, and studied the Fulani language in northern Cameroun. Each week Walter sent me a little blue aerogram written in German. (It was amazing how much German I learned in those two years!) In one he wrote:

> *Faith is a risk on God. Life is a risk on God. Love is a risk on God . . . All that we now experience will be used by the Lord in some way. Nothing will be in vain. The long darkness we endure will become illuminating lightnings; the separation will become a finding-again, more beautiful than ever. The salt will come into our testimony through the period we have to live through now — the period of separation, of certain uncertainty, of a blind flight in a definite direction . . . Let us work as*

if there would be no love and let us love as if there would be no work.

From my isolated mission station, I found that I could share honestly with Walter about my deepest problems as a young missionary. I told him how difficult it was to live in harmony with my co-worker, an older single lady. I had heard that the greatest missionary problem is the missionary herself. Now I had to admit it and face it. Walter comforted me greatly with these words:

> *It's not necessary for us always to fly. Then we would become proud and frivolous. For that reason it is God's grace when He gives us burdens to make us small. Only when we are small can we work for Him. If we are really humble, then such troubles will not make us unfruitful, but fruitful. The burdens are like the weights you find in old clocks. Without the weights the clock will not run. Think of 2 Corinthians 4:7: "We have this treasure in jars of clay to show that this all-surpassing power is from God and not from us."*
>
> *When we are told to bear one another's burdens in Galatians 6:2, this can mean not only the burden the other person has, but also which he is.*

Tests of Love

As I think back on our early days, I recall Walter's counsel to young people who came to him for advice. How could they test their love? How could they know whether they were mature enough to take the wedding vows and promise to stay together all their lives until they were parted by death? If sex is no test of love, what is the test? Here is what he proposed:[2]

First: *The sharing test.* Real love wants to share, to give, to reach out. It thinks of the other one, not of himself. When you read something, how often do you have the thought, *I would like to share this with my friend?* When you plan something, do you think of what you would like to do or what the other one would enjoy? The German author, Herman Oeser, put it this way: "Those who want to become happy should not marry. The important thing is to make the other one happy. Those who want to be understood should not marry. The important thing is to understand one's partner."

Second: *The strength test.* Real love should not take away your strength; instead it should give you new energy and strength. It should fill you with joy, make you creative, and motivate you more.

Third: *The respect test.* There is no real love without respect, without each being able to look up to the other one. How would you answer the questions, Do I want this young man to be the father of my children? Do I want this young woman to be the mother of my children? Am I proud of my partner?

Fourth: *The habit test.* Love accepts the other one with his habits. Don't marry on the installment plan, thinking that these things will change later on. Very likely they will not. You must accept the other one as he is now, including his habits and shortcomings. You should ask yourselves, Do we only love each other or do we also like each other?

Fifth: *The quarrel test.* When a couple come to me and want to get married, I always ask them if they have once had a real quarrel—not just a casual difference of opinion, but a real fight. The point is not the quarreling, but the ability to be reconciled to each other. This ability should be trained and tested before marriage. Not sex, but rather this quarrel test, is a profitable premarital experience. Are we able to forgive each other and to give in to each other?

Sixth: *The time test.* A year is the minimum. Two

years may be safer. There is an old saying: "Never get married until you have summered and wintered with your partner." In case you are in doubt about your feeling of love, time will tell. Ask yourselves, Has our love summered and wintered? Have we known each other long enough? When in doubt, don't.

Sex is no test of love. Love does not grow out of sex. It must grow into sex. This kind of love is built on trust, confidence, and fellowship. It calls for a reliable and lasting relationship. Premarital sex can hinder such love, because it so often brings guilt and pain.[3]

Certainty of Love

There are two things I have known for certain in my adult life: The first is that I am a child of God, and the second, that God called me to be the wife of Walter Trobisch. It meant giving up my own dreams, and yet it was the fulfillment of far more than I could have dreamed.

We became engaged "long distance" while I was still in Cameroun and Walter was in Germany. We were separated for almost two years in time and a continent in distance. In one of my letters to Walter during this time of separation I wrote:

Walter, I want to tell you why I love you. When I picture you in my mind, I can see you stretching out your hand to me. I trust your hand for it is the hand of a safe and secure man. It is true, you walk a little ahead of me, but when you realize I'm getting out of breath and can't quite keep up, you stand still. You turn around and give me your hand to help me over the hard places. Then I come very near to you and you talk to me and comfort me. You don't make fun of my thoughts.

What Makes a Marriage?

Through the years we recognized the truth of

Genesis 2:24, that marriage is based on three basic steps: leaving father and mother, cleaving to each other in love, and becoming one flesh.

1. *Leaving father and mother.* That definitive first step, leaving, is accomplished as the wedding, the official marriage ceremony, the legal act, is performed. If this does not take place, as we see so often when young couples just begin living together, then we have all the confusions and sicknesses that come from "the stolen marriage." For example, what about the child conceived in such a relationship? Or what about the young woman when her friend leaves her? Is she a "widow"?

Leaving means decisively cutting the cord which binds the young couple to their parents. I shall never forget what Walter's mother said to us and our guests as we gathered in our pastor's home the evening before our wedding. She stood up, barely five feet tall, and said in clear tones: "I hereby renounce the first place in my son's life and give that to Ingrid." She kept her word.

Through the years we realized more and more how important this step is as we saw marriages, world-wide, suffering because there had been no "leaving."

2. *Cleaving.* Many husbands and wives no longer have time for each other. The husband forgets to tell his wife that she is number one in his life. He gives the impression that other things are more important — his work, or maybe even just watching football. The wife may be engrossed in their new baby or in her career. This results in an empty marriage where the "chariot wheels grind heavily." There is sand in the gears. I tried to explain this to Walter in a letter once when he was away on a long trip:

> *There is a certain transfiguration when I can be completely one with you in body, mind and soul. This experience gives me the strength to overcome all the*

demands of our daily living, but this experience was with-held between your last trip and this new one. You were too busy. My heart grew heavier and heavier, so that I could hardly bear it. Then it was hard to let you go. Sometimes I think that these unfulfilled desires and hopes which cannot be separated from my heart and soul are a kind of sacrifice, a burnt offering, which makes the time together more fruitful.

Being able to express our feelings is the secret of cleaving in love. What a great experience it was for both Walter and me when we realized that feelings are neither right nor wrong. They just are. I could express my feelings to Walter, and, instead of being threatened by them and rushing to a defense with words like, "You shouldn't feel that way," he would say, "I understand. This is the way you feel." When I could name my feelings, he could help me tame them and get things back into focus.

I still have the meditation Walter wrote about love during the time of our engagement:

He who loves is no longer alone. The one he loves is constantly present with him. He renounces the right to remain at the center of his own life. He permits someone else to enter into the midst of it and senses that to be sweet fortune. He gives himself up and lets himself go. He be-comes empty like an open hand which holds nothing, but waits until something will be put into it. He who loves has the courage to become one who needs something.

Swiss psychiatrist Dr. Paul Tournier talks about the "dialogue of the deaf" when couples try to communicate with each other only by talking, but not by listening. Each turns a deaf ear to the other. Yet, to love means to listen. Sometimes we cannot listen to our partner, but only to our own cries. Women want to be comforted, while men look for understanding from their marriage partner. Each needs to be heard.

3. *Becoming one flesh.* Physical love is the most intimate sphere in the life of a married couple. Every man is different. Every woman is different. Therefore, every couple is doubly different, and a part of the fun of sexual love is the originality of each couple. It's a great freedom to remember that, as Charlie Shedd once said, "Sex is a twenty-year warm-up." A couple is truly free when they are released from their need to "perform" and can learn how to enjoy the pleasures of relaxed, easy sex! They can then forget about being spectators. They can let go completely and enjoy their sensations.

When God created man in His image, He created them as man and woman. He made Eve from the rib of her husband and brought her to him. Is there any better way to explain the great desire of husband and wife to become one flesh than that they came from one body?

Geborgenheit in Marriage

And that brings me to the subject of *Geborgenheit* in marriage. I have often told husbands that the greatest erogenous zone of the wife's body is her heart. Only what reaches the heart (usually through the ears) will enable the wife to be ready to give her all in the physical union, and to enable the husband to have fulfillment himself.

Dr. Bovet compares the love of the husband to a warm cloak. As long as the wife feels encircled, wrapped up in this cloak, she is able to surrender herself completely and unconditionally to her husband, both body and mind. In order to give her this feeling of being sheltered, the husband has to learn that it is not unmanly to express his feelings. If his words and caresses go together with the attitude of his heart, they will convey to her the message, "You are loved."

But often an unkindness, a reproach, or a harsh or

inconsiderate word can cause a hole in the cloak, where winds of discontent and fear blow through. Hurt and anger deprive the wife of the feeling of being sheltered and wrapped in his love and thus make it impossible for her to surrender completely in the physical union.

Silence does not mend holes. It is useless to try to heal a wounded heart by "having sex." The only way to mend it is to talk to each other and to share honestly about the hurts and to ask for mutual forgiveness. Anger undiscussed can become "frozen anger," a common cause for depression.

If a husband makes an effort to mend the holes in the cloak, the wife gains the confidence and basic trust so essential for surrender. Just as the bird entrusts itself to the air and the fish to the water, so will the wife be able to entrust herself to her husband.

This ability to give herself completely is her deepest secret. But in order to do this, she must first accept and love herself and genuinely be thankful for being a woman. This confidence in herself and complete trust in the sheltering love of her husband will enable her, figuratively speaking, to jump off a cliff without any doubt in her heart that her husband will be there to catch her. It is like learning to dive — a good illustration of what the wife experiences in the act of love. She dives into the deep water without hesitation. She is not afraid because she knows her loving husband is there waiting to receive her with open arms.[4]

The husband also needs to feel encircled by the warmth of his wife's body to find true *Geborgenheit*. One young husband expressed this desire in a birthday card he gave to his wife. It said, "There's only one thing nicer than having you close, and that is having you closer."

Self-Pity

Self-pity is poisonous to a marriage. Have you seen women (or men) who are "pouters"? People who like to throw a "pity-party" when they feel their partner has slighted them? Recently I talked to a troubled young couple. The wife had habitually locked herself in the bedroom when her feelings were hurt. She reasoned, "If my husband really loves me, then he will know why I am hurt even without any words."

I had to tell her the truth. "My friend, the poor man doesn't have a clue. He loves you very much, I know that, but you have to tell him when he has done something (or has forgotten to do something) which hurts you. *A baby has the right to be understood without words, but not a grown woman.*"

The Mystery of Marriage

One pastor I know tells the couples who come to him to be married, "If you want to get some idea of what your marriage will be like, you (pointing to the man) imagine *your* father married to *her* mother." The pastor then points to the woman and says, "Now imagine *your* father married to *his* mother." This never fails to bring an interesting response.

There is no such thing as a perfect marriage. The imperfections of marriage keep us humble. the safest way to become humble about one's virtues is to get married. Even when a person has consciously rejected the style or personality of his own parent, there still remains a strong influence. Each one of us is our parents' child and that is the raw material we bring into a marriage. On the wedding day a couple has, as it were, two heaps of raw material on a vacant lot and they have to build a marriage out of those piles. That is hard work. It means accepting yourself and your partner, with all the rough edges.

Marriage is not a goal, but a journey. Besides being the leaving, cleaving and becoming one flesh described before, marriage is a mystery. Mike Mason in *The Mystery of Marriage* says:

> Love convinces a couple that they are the greatest romance that has ever been, that no two people have ever loved as they do, and that they will sacrifice absolutely anything in order to prove it. Marriage is the down-to-earth dimension of romance, the translation of a romantic blueprint into costly reality.[5]

The apostle Paul wrote that marriage "is a profound mystery—but I am talking about Christ and the church" (Ephesians 5:32). Marriage is like looking into a mirror. When we look at Christ's love, we can see a picture of how God wants husband and wife to live together. And when they live together according to God's will, their marriage becomes the mirror, reflecting Christ's love. This mystery is great.

Tapping Your Hidden Strength

1. What does the author's view that "marriage should be a calling" mean to you?

2. If you are single and dating: How does your love stand up to the six-part test in this chapter? If you are married: How does your married love stand up to the first five parts? What areas could use improvement? What are three specific commitments you can make to improve the weak areas of your love?

3. Review the three essential elements of marriage in Genesis 2:24. A popular speaker on marriage has said that practically all marital problems can be traced to a violation of one of these three elements. Do you agree or disagree? Why?

4. The author states, "Marriage is not a goal, but a journey." What should this mean to young couples today?

CHAPTER 7

Bearing Children

How planned conception strengthens the marriage

In looking back over my life, I can see that my children have been my greatest teachers—and I am still in the learning process.

The first lesson I had to learn was the fact that I might never have a child, but that a marriage is full and complete even without children. God's three-step definition of marriage in Genesis 2:24 makes no mention of children. Children are indeed a blessing of God, but they are an additional blessing.

Today one in five couples have difficulty in the conception and bearing of a child. A generation ago it was one in ten. There are many reasons for this increasing number, including physical problems, the postponement of the time for child-bearing, and the use of oral contraceptives over a long period of time. Dr. Rudolf Vollman, one of the world's greatest medical authorities on the menstrual cycle, says that using oral contraceptives is like using "a sledgehammer to kill a flea."

I believe that the greatest moment in the life of a

couple is when they can knowingly conceive a new life. At this moment, they are one with their creator. And I also believe that it is possible, with the scientific knowledge at our disposal, to teach couples to recognize the signs of the wife's fertile time and to live in harmony with them. This is a great source of hidden strength in the marriage relationship and one well worth studying. For more complete information regarding fertility, see my book, *The Joy of Being a Woman.*[1]

A young married couple who had struggled with childlessness for over a decade unexpectedly were able to adopt a child. The mother expressed their joy in a letter to her adopted son. It is a deep heart expression from one unable to give natural birth. She graciously has given me permission to share it with you.

> Little one,
> How precious in our sight you are.
> Do you know you are a miracle?
> Do you know that your breathing,
> your bouncing,
> your bright eyes and smile
> are evidence of God's goodness to you
> in granting you life?
> Each day, we are in awe
> that you are with us—
> that you are ours—
> that you are in our family.
> You have come in an unpredictable,
> uncalculated,
> unplanned,
> unforseen . . . (to us) . . . way.
> God has known you from the beginning and preserved your coming forth. He has given you life and connected you to us in this ordained way, apart from any effort on our part to secure you, other than our willing "yes, we'll take him!"

Little one,
 We have welcomed you with great joy,
  confounding our many speculations
   about adoption.
 We feel certain your smiles reflect
  our great joy in you.

But, little one,
 Will you ever understand why our joy is so great?
 It is because great sadness was first in its place.

Will you someday fathom our tears, our hurting hearts, our mental anguish and our spiritual discouragement over being childless in a world of easily fertile people?

Will you someday sense the tough reality of unending monthly frustration with an imperfect body that doesn't perform as it was meant to when we've counted on being able to reproduce?

Will you someday realize the medical, financial, social and emotional consequences we choose to experience as we repeatedly remind God that we're available, if He would choose to create life through us?

Will you ever sense the nagging doubt, even as we play, that you may never share playtime with a brother or sister because adoption is not an easy option these days, because we are not getting any younger, and because our medical options are looking grim?

Little one,
 Will you ever fully know how much we've
  wanted you?

Little one,
 The trial of infertility is still with us — even as we hold and cuddle you — we are not classified as a fertile couple. But by God's grace, we are your parents.

You are "fleshy" evidence that God *is* "working all things out for the good of those who love Him and are called according to His purpose" . . . of conforming us "to the likeness of His Son."

His purpose is not ultimately for us to be fertile or for us to be parents.
His purpose is for us to be like Jesus.
Certainly you, little one, will be used by God in our lives to teach us to be like Jesus.
Already you have taught us a depth of love we didn't know possible.

We are thankful and thrilled you are here.
We are also mindful of the unknown ahead in our relationship with you.

By grace you have come to us,
    by grace we will each proceed
        to love and care for you in Jesus' name.

Little one,
    Will you someday grasp the full meaning of God's grace in your coming to our family?

Little one,
    Will you someday grasp the full meaning of God's ultimate grace in His willingness to adopt you into His family?

It is a miracle that you are ours . . .
    but a far greater one that you can be His.

The Miracle of Childbirth

Walter and I struggled through the verdict of doctors who did not give us much hope of becoming parents. But I found great comfort in the story of Hannah in 1 Samuel 1 and 2. Hannah was stubborn in her prayer life and didn't give up. Her praise song, *My heart rejoices in the LORD*, was even repeated by Mary when she knew she was to be the mother of our Savior.

I underlined in my Bible that little sentence of 1 Samuel 2:21 (KJV): "And the LORD visited Hannah, so that she conceived, and bare three sons and two daughters." I was in my thirtieth year of life when our first child, Katrine, was born. After her birth, God gave us the joy of having three sons, Daniel, David and Stephen, and our youngest daughter Ruth.

"Childbirth should be the hour of a woman's greatest dignity," said Dr. Pierre Vellay, pioneer in the field of natural childbirth. "It should be a real step forward, not only in the liberation of the woman, but also in the liberation of the couple."

Wherever Walter and I taught Family Life Seminars throughout the world, we placed strong emphasis on natural childbirth, with the husband's active participation, as an avenue of emotional and spiritual enrichment in the marriage. One husband, after supporting his wife during the hours of labor and being present at the birth of their child, wrote: "I shall never forget the joy of that moment, even if I live to be a thousand years old!"

"Childbirth — for the joy of it!" is the slogan of a couples' organization in the Los Angeles area. If the whole experience of childbirth can be remembered with joy, it is carried over in the attitude of the parents toward the child.

Doula — Mothering the Mother

I have a good friend who lives in Germany, who became a widow after two years of marriage. Reinhild never had a child of her own. Each week during my first pregnancy, she wrote to me. Although we were separated by continents (I was at a bush station in northern Cameroun), I felt her loving support during that time. I once asked her, "How does one learn how to love?"

Her response was, "By letting yourself be loved."

At no time is this emotional need greater for a young mother than during the months of pregnancy, the time of childbirth, breastfeeding and then during the years of coping with young children. I like to use the word *doula* for this ministry. It comes from the Greek word *doulos* which means "servant." In this instance a *doula* can mean "someone who mothers the mother." I was very thankful for a supportive husband, but also for Reinhild, my German friend, who took this position of *doula* in my life, not only during my first pregnancy but in all the succeeding ones. Her love was a visible form of Christ's love at a time when I desperately needed it.

I am happy to hear of active congregations where older women are mothering the young mother. The older women take food during those first critical days after the mother comes home with her new baby, or once a week they help the new mother "come up for air" by taking over the children while she goes out by herself.

Recently I was invited to speak to an active women's group which meets the second Tuesday of every month. The mothers come with their young children. A group of older women take care of the children and cook lunch, while the young women have an uninterrupted time of Bible study and sharing. After lunch, when the young women leave with their children, the older women have their Bible study. Needless to say, this is a growing congregation.

Martin Luther said, "When you see a child, you see Jesus Christ." Didn't Jesus Himself say, "Whoever receives one such child in my name, receives me" (Matthew 18:5, RSV)? The chief of the stalwart Chagga tribe, who lived on the slopes of Kilimanjaro where I was born, told his men: "Take good care of the pregnant woman. She is the most important person in our tribe." What would happen in our society if we would follow his advice?

Mother Maintenance

Recently I read an article in a church bulletin entitled, "Mother Maintenance," and, with the author's permission, I want to share it with you. William E. Keller wrote:

Many of us take better care of our cars than we do of our mothers, and yet we only expect our cars to last five or six years but we expect our mothers to last a lifetime. Maybe we need a maintenance manual for mothers so we would know how to take care of them, at least as well as we do our automobiles.

Engine: A mother's engine is one of the most dependable kinds you can find. She can reach top speed from a prone position at a single cry from a sleeping child. But regular breaks are needed to keep up that peak performance. Mothers need a hot bath and a nap every 100 miles, a baby-sitter and a night out every 1,000 miles, and a live-in baby-sitter with a one-week vacation every 10,000 miles.

Battery: Mother's batteries should be recharged regularly. Handmade items, notes, unexpected hugs and kisses and frequent "I love you's" will do very nicely.

Carburetor: When a mother's carburetor floods it should be treated immediately with Kleenex and a soft shoulder.

Brakes: See that she uses her brakes to slow down often and come to a full stop occasionally.

Fuel: Most mothers can run indefinitely on coffee, leftovers and salads, but an occasional dinner for two at a nice restaurant will really add to her efficiency.

Chassis: Mothers function best when their bodies are properly maintained. Regular exercise should be encouraged and provided for as necessary. A change in hairdo or makeup in spring and fall are also helpful. If you notice the chassis beginning to sag, immediately start a program of walking, jogging, swimming or bike riding. These are most effective when done with fathers.

Tune-ups: Mothers need regular tune-ups. Compliments are both the cheapest and the most effective way to keep a mother purring contentedly.

Tapping Your Hidden Strength

1. Do you agree with the author that a marriage can be full and complete even without children? Why or why not?

2. Name at least six specific emotional needs that a young mother faces during pregnancy and then during the first year of motherhood.

3. Does your church have an organized program to "mother the young mothers"? Identify six ways in which you and your friends could help new mothers in your church or neighborhood. Talk with your pastor about organizing an ongoing *doula* program as part of your church's ministry.

CHAPTER 8

Blending Family and Ministry

The "Questionnaire of God"—ten areas to explore

In the last year of Walter's life, a friend asked him, "If you were to do it over again, what would you change in your life and ministry?"

"I would keep my home my home," he answered. He explained what he meant: "I would not put the burden on my family of accepting counselees into our intimate family circle."

It seemed that our family was always "extended" and there were few meals without a guest at our table. Many lives were changed because of this, but it was hard for me to accept at times. It was not easy for our children either, although their school friends were often the guests who enlarged our family circle.

At times we were the visitors, and then others experienced the same problem. I remember one little girl, the daughter of a hospitable German pastor and his wife, who said to her father as we were finishing a meal together, "On Christmas Eve it will just be our family, won't it, Daddy? You promised, remember?" I knew exactly how she felt.

When I look back now though, I am deeply thankful that we had an open home, and that we learned the joy of hospitality as a family. We were enriched as we often "entertained angels unaware," spoken of in Hebrews 13:2. In our little home nestled in a hamlet on the Lichtenberg, heaven sometimes came down when someone made a new commitment to Christ, or a young couple received new strength to live their marriage. The same still happens as I share my home, *Geborgenheit*, in the Ozarks.

Recently I was reassured of the importance of having an open home when I reread this note in my "tree album," a special little book containing my collection of tree pictures and their accompanying thoughts. A young American woman, who had just finished a term in Taiwan where she taught English at the university, visited us on the Lichtenberg, and she wrote:

> *I think you don't know how much staying — living with you in your home — meant to me. Maybe you've heard it before, but the house alone seems to have a special peace and warmth surrounding it.*
>
> *The Lord always knows where we are — physically and spiritually — and He knows our needs. But what's more, He knows how to fill them.*
>
> *This past year I felt as if I were walking through a desert, with only the water and supplies I collected and built up before my journey. God had even warned me that it wasn't going to be an easy trip. He equipped me with all I needed and then said, "When you run out, you only have* Me."
>
> *But then I went to Taiwan. Wow, did that wilderness ever get dry and lonely and full of holes, sand, weeds, bugs. I now know what it's like to be without the overflowing water. The hardest part was* not *knowing if I would ever come to the green spots again.*

How could I ever have doubted God's grace and love? Little did I know that on this trip I would walk right into an oasis — the Lichtenberg. The food, the rest, the water, the breeze — what strength I gained by that oasis! I loved to sit and listen to you talk — about anything, because it seems that each word became a pondering thought to me. I don't think I have ever used such little time to learn so much, not only about truth and other people, but also about myself. What is my ministry?

Tell me one thing, Ingrid, did all of your beautiful, precious flowers also used to be weeds?

The Risks of Taking Guests

Taking guests into our home for several days at a time had its risks. I well remember one young woman in her late twenties who had written to us for help. We replied faithfully to her letters. One day Walter said to me, "It is time that we invite Miriam [not her real name] to come and visit us. She needs to have some personal talks. Are you in agreement?"

Our little house was already bursting with our children and Mutti, Walter's mother, who was now an invalid and needed constant care, so it was with a little reluctance that I agreed we could invite Miriam. She could stay in a guest room available at our neighbor's home and take her meals with us.

Miriam arrived. Although she was a teacher and had helped many children, she had received little help herself. Walter rearranged his writing schedule so that he could spend an hour with her every day before lunch. He assigned her reading (we both believed in bibliotherapy) and she plowed through her questions of faith and personal commitment. One day when I called my family to lunch, Miriam did not come.

"Walter, is she sick?" I asked.

"Not really," he said, "but I think it would be well if you would take a tray to her room. She has something to tell you."

We finished our meal. I prepared the tray and knocked on Miriam's door. She was in tears.

"What's the matter, Miriam?" I asked.

"Something terrible."

"Can you tell me about it?"

She blurted it out. "Mrs. Trobisch, I'm in love with your husband."

My heart went out to Miriam. She was one of a whole generation of young women in Germany who had to grow up without fathers after World War II. Because of all the men who had died in that war, the ratio was one man for seven women. Other young women, like Miriam, grew up with cold and distant fathers. Walter, a fatherly man, had taken her seriously, listened to her problems, affirmed and complimented her. It was almost a part of the healing process that she make this transference of her affections — and from there, eventually, find the way to her loving heavenly Father. I had been through it myself — in my own struggles as a teenage fatherless daughter.

I was able to set Miriam's heart at rest and say, "I can understand how you feel, Miriam. I love Walter too."

Miriam and I became good friends after that and, when it was time for her to leave, she asked, "May I stay on and help you? I still have a few days of vacation before the next school term and I see that you have a lot to do."

She took turns with us keeping vigil at Mutti's bedside and was with her for a few hours just before Mutti's peaceful death. Then Miriam stayed on and helped us prepare for the funeral.

"Now I am not afraid of death," Miriam said, "for I have seen a Christian die."

Because of Walter's mix of family and ministry, Miriam was able to go on and become a mature Christian woman with a ministry of her own.

Quality or Quantity Time?

And what about the children? How did we find time for them in a busy ministry of writing and teaching? For us there was no magic formula—like having *quality* time instead of *quantity* time. I am convinced that children also need quantity time. That is why I felt my children had top priority as babies and preschoolers, and I was very jealous of keeping that time with them. In each case, my child and I learned to work together as a team during the good experience of breastfeeding. That deep unity, learned in the early months as a "nursing couple," carried over into childhood and even later.

When our children were of school age and after Mutti's death, I accompanied Walter on one of his teaching trips to Africa each year. That meant separation from the children, and we tried to make it up to them on our family camping trips in the summer. We had some hilarious experiences, traveling in two small Volkswagens with two tents and all the camping equipment necessary for seven people. Our family even went to Sweden where we traced my Swedish roots. Wonder of wonders, when we came home, we were still friends.

I overheard a conversation recently between my son Stephen and his uncle, a busy pastor in a large suburban area. Stephen complained, "My parents were often on trips when I was a child."

His uncle replied, "Stephen, I didn't go on any trips; I was always at home. Yet for my children, I was never at home. When your parents were at home, they were *at home.*"

I often tell my children that we did the best we could. Now they should learn from our mistakes and go and do better.

The Search for Geborgenheit

I asked a young man Stephen's age, who was having problems both at home and at school, "Where do you feel safe and secure? Where do you find real *Geborgenheit?*"

"When I'm in my Volkswagen Beetle," he answered without hesitation. "That's the only place I really feel sheltered and *geborgen.* It belongs to me."

My youngest daughter, Ruth, was becoming aware of the need for a sense of shelter and safety, and one Christmas vacation she announced that she had invited twenty-two friends to spend the New Year's weekend with us. They wanted to have a retreat together and had already planned the menu and where they would sleep—some of them at neighboring farms. They would sit on the floor in our living room for the meetings. "Everything will work out, Mother," she said enthusiastically, "just as long as you remain calm and I remain calm."

"What is your theme?" I asked.

I was pleased when Ruth answered, *"Geborgenheit.* Actually, that was Stephen's idea. He may be only my brother, but he's pretty sharp. He says that's what all the young people are looking for—a place where they are safe."

We had a great time that weekend. Walter wasn't with us because he was speaking at a large youth gathering in Minneapolis. But Ruth asked her oldest brother, Daniel, to talk about his studies on prenatal psychology, the healing of birth traumas and memories and, above all, how they could be avoided.

I was to tell how mothers can give their small children the feeling of *Geborgenheit*. We each had to draw a sketch of the place where we felt *geborgen* and the place where we felt no *Geborgenheit*. For the latter I drew a picture of my cluttered desk.

Immediately the young people sent me to my room to straighten up my desk, for, they said, "we cannot continue our retreat if our mother does not feel sheltered and *geborgen.*" I shall always be grateful for their insight. One of the times family and ministry came together for me was at that retreat. Through my children's ministry, I learned better how to manage my own. I have discovered that whenever I have a major battle ahead of me in the Kingdom of God, I must begin by making order in my inner self and then around me.

Inner Order

To work on the inner order, it is well to look into God's mirror, the Ten Commandments. Pastor Herbert Fuchs, who married Walter and me and who was Walter's mentor and soul counselor, put the Ten Commandments in modern language and called it "The Questionnaire of God." Here is the English translation:

1. Which person or what thing is more important to you than God? What do you think about the first thing in the morning and the last thing at night?

2. Are you guided in your thinking and actions by superstitious ideas? Do fortune-tellers, horoscopes, spiritism and magic arts influence your life or those who live with you?

3. When you make plans and decisions do you seek God's will? Do you take enough time to listen to God's Word, or do you try to escape it through work and pleasure?

4. With whom do you have strained relationships? Within or outside your family, are there those to whom you are indifferent or toward whom you feel reproach and scorn? Are you ready to take responsibility over and above your personal field of activity?

5. Is there someone who may have wronged you and whom you cannot forgive and then forget [the problem]? Do you try to help others outwardly or inwardly, or do you look for help only for yourself?

6. Is God's commandment the standard for you in sexual questions, not only in relationship with others but also in regard to yourself? Where do you see the root of your failure in this field?

7. Have you illegally taken something for your own or not returned something which you borrowed? What do you possess that you don't really need, but that someone else needs badly? Does God receive His share of your earnings?

8. To whom have you lied? Whom have you judged deliberately, falsely or unkindly, either by written or spoken word?

9. Whom do you secretly envy because of his or her personal appearance, reputation, position, abilities or possessions? Can you rejoice with someone who has more than you, or do you become bitter when you compare yourself with such a person?

10. Are you ready to receive everything as entrusted to you from God, even that which you do not understand and which is not according to your personal desires? Do the words "good luck" and "bad luck" occur in your vocabulary?

When I first considered these questions, I wrote down my answers to each one and then went to an older woman, my prayer partner, who could counsel me spiritually. She assured me of Christ's words, "He who comes to me, I will not cast out." She reminded me of the promise in 1 John 1:9: "If we confess our sins, he is faithful and just and will forgive us our sins."

I went on my way with a new inner strength and sense of authority to help others as I had been helped. Walter and I repeatedly followed these guidelines to inner order in our spiritual lives. In addition to carefully reviewing these concepts, we made restitution an important part of "repairing the cut-off telephone wires" in our communication with God. That seemed to cement in place the other things.

Table Talk

One of the greatest influences in a child's life is the conversation that goes on around the dining room table. In East Germany we once visited Wittenberg and saw the home of Martin Luther where he and his family often shared meals with students. The down-to-earth conversations that took place at those times are recorded in *Luther's Table Talks,* and undoubtedly contributed greatly to molding the spiritual lives of those students.

What do you talk about at your meals? Some parents use the time at the table to teach their children correct table manners. That is good, but it's not enough.

In my childhood home, every evening after supper my father read from a Bible story book. Then we sang together. One of our favorites was the Swedish song:

> Children of the heavenly Father
> Safely in His bosom gather,
> Nestling bird nor star in heaven
> Such a refuge ne'er was given.

Then we held hands and prayed our evening prayer

together. We learned as a family what my parents had first practiced as a couple: *to become one in spirit before God.* This is one way you could help your children establish the deepest roots of their *Geborgenheit.*

At a retreat for U.S. servicemen and their families in England, I shared the importance of table talk. An unmarried Air Force pilot came to me afterward and said, "I can't remember any time in my childhood when we sat down together as a family. My father worked nights and my mother days. There was always some food on the back burner, but no family celebrations."

I smiled gently, touched his hand and said, "Now you know how you will do it differently when you are married."

There should be a lot of laughter and games in a family, too. I don't know of anything better to relieve the inevitable tension that comes when people live under the same roof. A teenager who was having trouble with his parents (good friends of ours) told them one day at the table, "If we couldn't all laugh together around this table, I wouldn't be able to stand this family." Love and laughter hold us together.

Jonathan Edwards, that great colonial theologian, once said, "Every family ought to be a little church, consecrated to Christ and wholly influenced and governed by His rules." At least one biblical couple successfully blended family and ministry. In 1 Corinthians 16:19, Paul says to the church in Corinth: "Aquila and Priscilla greet you warmly in the Lord, and so does the church that meets at their house."

Tension Between Ministry and Family

Recently I attended the funeral of a good friend who had served as a missions director in his church. His daughter told how he visited her every day over a period of weeks as she recovered from a serious operation. "He drove sixty miles after a hard day's work at the office," she said, "but he came faithfully. His children were a part of his mission."

One of his sons, now following in his footsteps, put it this way, "Tension never existed between his ministry and his family."

If we could just learn that our families and our ministry are not in competition! There is time for both. Just as we must teach our children to prolong their tolerance level and not to demand instant gratification for their every desire, we must also teach them how to balance family and ministry.

My good friend Becky Pippert recognizes that need and has found her answer. She is a wife and mother as well as a speaker and author. In an interview in *Partnership* magazine (July-August 1987) she said, "My biggest struggle as a mom is balancing priorities because I have chosen to work part time . . . Speaking means that I'm away from the children, and I have decided to limit myself to two or three overnights a month . . . I have no doubt that my primary goal is to be a wife and a mother. And I do feel very, very strongly that women are to be a great help to their husbands. But when I get to heaven, God is not going to ask me what I did with my husband's gifts."

Now that I can look back on these years, I wonder what I would do differently in combining family and ministry. I still believe that people come before programs and projects. I am happy now that we shared our home with so many. Those young people who lived with us and were included in our extended family are now carrying on our vision of "releasing couple power" throughout the world. (We'll talk more about "couple power" in chapter 11.) One thing that I have learned is that we never lose by giving, as we read in Proverbs 11:24,25:

One man gives freely, yet gains even more;
    another withholds unduly, but comes to poverty.
A generous man will prosper;
    he who refreshes others will himself be refreshed.

What would I do? Probably just more of the same, but with increased self-confidence, and certainly more open communication.

Tapping Your Hidden Strength

1. Are you confident that each of your children regards your home as a place of security and shelter from the stresses of life? In what ways can you help him or her find and enjoy *Geborgenheit* in your home?

2. Go through "The Ten Commandments Questionnaire" beginning on page 85 to check on your inner order. Ask God to guide you in confessing to Him any areas where you have fallen short of His standard.

3. Is the dinner table a fun place for your family? In what ways can you make family time around the table more enjoyable, meaningful and memorable?

CHAPTER 9

Handling the Loss of a Love

Nine signs of recovery

"It pays to suffer lover's grief," Walter wrote in his little book, *Love Is a Feeling to be Learned.* "Suffering is not something to be eliminated, regardless of the cost. If we live through it and accept it, suffering can become a spring of riches, of depth, growth and fulfillment—yes, of happiness."[1]

Loss of a Friend

An aborted friendship, painful as it may be, can become a source of hidden strength, once the wounds are healed. We must avoid the process of suberization, developing a lot of corky, scarred tissue in our heart wounds. Frustration comes when love is not returned, and that can be a great blow to one's self-image. It takes great strength to stand tall at a time of being rejected.

It reminds me of the statement of a mountain climber who said, "The trick to life is not to win—it's to get back up when you lose, and try again."

Sometimes our pain comes not from an aborted friendship, but from a friendship run dry. A dry cistern takes the place of a deep well. After the initial attraction has worn off, only emptiness remains.

Dr. Marion Hilliard, who wrote *A Woman Doctor Looks at Love and Life,* frankly tells the story of her own disappointment in love. Before her early death, Dr. Hilliard was the Chief of Obstetrics and Gynecology at a large Canadian hospital and wrote many popular articles on women and marriage. One day she received an indignant visitor in her office.

"Just what makes you think you're an expert on marriage?" the visitor snapped at Dr. Hilliard. "You're single!"

"I kept a straight face," Dr. Hilliard said, "and then pointed out to her, 'Being single gives me an objective point of view. A married woman only knows one man. I know a lot about marriage, though I've never experienced it, because I have listened to the problems of literally thousands of married women.'"

Missing Out on Love

She maintained her professionalism with her visitor as she added, "I also know, even better, the problems of unmarried women. I learned that the bitterest renunciation of all she makes is not a mate—it is motherhood. Looking back on my life, I can chart those moments that were pivotal. The most crucial was the date I had one evening with a man I loved.

"He was an engineer and had been away on a project for several months. I was interning and missed him dreadfully. There was a tacit understanding that we were engaged. Together we would plan our future and set a date.

"He called for me, looking brown and handsome. He had even borrowed a car. We went to dinner—I adored it—dinner away from the hospital was always a thrill. Replete, cozy in the car, waiting for my moment, while he talked of love I fell asleep. I had been on duty in the delivery room for four successive nights preceding this. He drove me home, wakened me, and said a curt good night. How thankful I've always been for that catnap. A short time later he married someone else. He then provided me with my Gethsemane: He asked me to be his wife's doctor and deliver their first baby. It was a valuable experience. Nothing else in my lifetime has ever or will ever hurt so much. On Mother's Day, in the early morning, that I might miss no overtone of human longing or resignation, the child was born. If I could accept that and survive — and I could — then I could withstand anything."[2]

A relationship may seem right. There is a "falling in love," (not to be confused with the "choosing to love" which is the basis of a lifelong commitment in marriage), but eventually the relationship may fall apart. On a TV program, one woman described it vividly: "The room that we were in came to a silent stop. The walls caved in around us . . . " What had she done wrong? Had she gone to sleep when she should have been awake? Had she served him cold pancakes when they should have been piping hot? She had given her best, but it was not good enough.

Love is a two-way street. The French writer, Albert Camus, says about these feelings of loss and uncertainty, "The astonishing or unfortunate thing is [they] bring us the cure at the same time they give rise to pain. Once we have accepted the fact of loss, we understand that the loved one obstructed a whole corner of the possible, pure now as a sky washed by rain" (from *Cahier II: Youthful Writings*, publisher unknown).

Signs of Recovery

In Robin Norwood's book entitled *Women Who Love Too Much*,[3] the author suggests nine signs of recovery after the loss of a love:

1. A woman must accept herself fully — "to be nobody else."

2. She accepts others as they are without trying to change them to meet her needs.

3. She is in touch with her feelings about every aspect of her life [including] sexual.

4. She cherishes herself including her body. (May I add, she must also learn to separate her feelings of self-worth from her body weight.)

5. Her self-esteem is great enough that she can enjoy being with others — especially men. She does not need to be needed in order to feel worthy.

6. She asks, "Is the relationship good for my growth?"

7. When a relationship is destructive, she is able to let go without experiencing disabling depression.

8. She values her serenity.

9. She knows that a relationship has to be between partners who share similar values, interests and goals and who have a capacity for intimacy.

Love's Power

In *Man and Woman He Made Them,* Jean Vanier tells of a tender relationship between Christine and Lawrence, each with a slight mental handicap. Lawrence had come to the institution full of anger and violence.

In approaching him with tenderness, Christine awakened his heart. It was astonishing to see, in the space of a few months, the change which took place in him. He became more gentle, more calm; his face became peaceful and relaxed; at table, he would listen to others; all his ag-

gression seemed to have melted away . . . When Christine dropped him, Lawrence fell into depression; he closed in on himself again . . . but it was amazing to have seen the beauty of his heart. Loved in his being as a man, he had been transformed, although, unhappily, only for a time. Love is the most beautiful reality, but a reality which can also be very dangerous if it is not founded on a true commitment.

Vanier then warns of stepping into the sexual expression of such a love. He is a French Christian, and his words are prophetic for us. He says:

> The sexual life, *if it is not lived in a covenant given by God,* can obscure the heart, render it opaque. Sexuality can be a sacrament of relationship, but it also can be the death of relationship. The kiss can obstruct the word, that word which is absolutely necessary to deepen the relationship. The sexual instinct is so powerful that it can carry a couple to physical union without going through the stages of friendship and sharing needed in order to know each other. Such a union has no solid foundation on which the future can be built.[4]

Divorce

Painful as it is, the loss of a love through a broken relationship or broken engagement is far less traumatic than the experience of a divorce. How much better when the disillusionment comes before the final commitment of marriage. Then the emotion can be like the one expressed in the old Scottish ballad:

> Lay me down and bleed a while
> Though I am wounded, I am not slain . . .
> I shall rise and fight again.

In *I Married You,* Walter explains to his audience the meaning of the biblical phrase "to cleave":

> The literal sense of the Hebrew word for "to cleave" is to stick to, or to be glued to a person. The hus-

band and wife are glued together like two pieces of paper. If you try to separate two pieces of paper which are glued together, you tear them both. If you try to separate husband and wife who cleave together, both are hurt — and in those cases where they have children, the children as well. Divorce means to take a saw and to saw apart each child, from head to toe, right through the middle.[5]

"As long as there is a breath of life in a marriage, I will fight for it," Walter used to say. When a couple is fighting, that is a good sign, for it means that they care. I remember when an African couple came to our home to settle a dispute. In his anger the husband had bitten off the ear lobe of his wife. Walter quieted them and assured them that there was great love between them. If the couple had been silent and indifferent to each other's feelings, Walter would have been much more concerned. The couple made up and went happily on their way after a short time.

In a marriage where there is no breath of life, it may be that the only thing to do is to sign the death certificate. But we must support the couple who goes through the pain of a divorce, a pain which is often greater than that of widowhood.

Recently a reader of our books wrote to me:

I have been shattered by Christian divorces. Why and how can it happen to Christians? Sometimes I fear that it could happen to me. Is a Christian marriage a guarantee that there will never be a divorce? And once love is lost, how is it restored between two people?

My answer to her was:

Life has no guarantees other than God's continuing love and our redemption through His Son. Christians are exposed to life's temptations just as non-Christians are. They experience the same peaks and valleys in their emotions and feelings as those who have never become acquainted with Jesus Christ. A Christian man may wake

up one morning, look at his wife and wonder, Why did I
ever choose her as my mate? Likewise, his wife may think,
I hardly know this man. How can he be my husband?

We have to look beyond ourselves. The fountain of
our love must always be Christ. "For with you is the fountain of life; in your light we see light" (Psalm 36:9). He is
our hidden strength and the source of all love. Our roots
are watered and we can claim for our marriages the
promises of Psalm 92:12-14:

> The righteous will flourish like a palm tree . . .
> planted in the house of the Lord . . .
> They will still bear fruit in old age,
> they will stay fresh and green.

In their marriage ceremony, one bride and groom
promised loyalty and fidelity to each other "so long as we
both shall love." A more accurate wording would have been
"so long as we both feel love." This is not the love based on
commitment that Christ spoke of when He stressed dying
to ourselves and becoming servants to one another.

Shortly after Walter and I were married, I made this
entry in my journal: "Marriage is to be experienced only
when the possibility of divorce doesn't exist." Many would
say this is unrealistic. We live in an imperfect world, therefore divorce is sometimes necessary. Perhaps. But the need
for divorce is not as great as statistics show it to be happen-
ing. And Christians need to be the first ones to stand up
and say so.

In a recent study of divorced couples, Dr. Mavis
Hetherington, professor of psychology at the University of
Virginia, revealed that "after one year of divorce, 60 percent of the men and 73 percent of the women felt they had
made a mistake. Even those who thought their marriages
had been terrible were saying that maybe they could have
worked their marital problems out." These people were

realizing that their need for love was greater than their need for divorce.

My niece Ann and her husband Bob were divorced after they had been married for seven years. Without going into the sad details of that eighteen-month period, I will jump ahead and say that today they have been happily remarried to each other for more than seven years.

How did this happen? Ann writes:

> I am still in awe when I consider what God has accomplished in our lives. Bob and I were talking together one spring-filled Sunday afternoon. It was a beautiful day. All at once, life seemed unbearably wonderful. After the pain of the past I was happy again. Finally I asked Bob how he thought the love between us had been restored. Without hesitating, he looked me straight in the eye and said, "Ann, the love between us was never gone."

> Never gone?! I silently protested. You must not have felt the same way I did!

> But slowly the significance of his words sank in. The love we had for one another was not of our own making. It was a gift from God. Through immaturity, through neglect of our foremost responsibility, that of nurturing our personal relationship with our creator, we had eventually destroyed all positive feelings we had for one another and all happiness we shared. The more we struggled to find that happiness, the more it eluded us. Yet it wasn't the love that was gone. It was the expression and emotion of love.

Restoring Love

The first step in restoring love is making a commitment to Jesus Christ who said, "As the Father has loved me, so have I loved you. Now remain in my love" (John 15:9). The next step is to make a lifetime commitment to your spouse. It must be free from conditions.

Then the labor of love must begin. Communication has top priority. Author John Powell once said that it takes the "rawest kind of courage" to reveal oneself openly and honestly to another — we all fear rejection.

In order to be understood, we must be understanding. We have two ears and one mouth, which means we should listen twice as much as we talk. Some communication experts believe that people listen at only 25 percent or less of their capacity.

There are four kinds of listening to keep in mind:

1. listening of superiority

2. listening of indifference

3. listening for the moment that others will stop speaking

4. listening and learning

There is no substitute for a good listener largely because there are so few of them. If you can become this kind of person to your spouse, chances are excellent your spouse will reciprocate. Then a life-giving channel of communication will always be open to you.

We must also learn to accept and appreciate our spouses for who they are. You can never change your mate. You can only change yourself.

There is not a married person alive who has not found at least one idiosyncrasy in his or her mate that he or she wishes were not there. The question is, Does it affect the quality of your marriage, or is it something you can learn to live with? If it is a serious problem that you have tried to work out but without success, go to work alleviating it by first laying it before the Lord. Second, look for a Christian counselor or pastor who could advise you. If the problem is still there, take a chance. Communicate it to your mate. Use a loving and accepting approach. If you feel counseling is necessary, ask your mate to go with you because you need him there.

A woman in her late twenties told me about an extremely difficult time in her marriage. She said, "I keep asking myself, *What am I doing here? Why do I hang on?* We'd both be much better off if we split. At least we would be happier."

She was experiencing the devil's lie: "It feels true, so it must be true."

Others say, "If it feels good, do it."

In this particular case, my friend hung on. Sometimes she felt like a hypocrite. Other times she was terribly depressed. But her loyalty won through and today she is extremely happy that she didn't follow her feelings.

So as long as there is a breath of life in the marriage, fight for it. Christian marriages are different only when they are centered on the "heavenly bridegroom" — the great servant — the one who said, "What therefore God hath joined together, let not man put asunder" (Matthew 19:6, KJV).

Loss Through Death

The loss of a spouse through death has been listed as the greatest cause of stress. I think this has to be qualified. A "good" death, if there is such a thing, can cause less stress than a divorce, because there is a clear-cut wound which has more promise of healing than the wound constantly opened up when one's former spouse is still alive. Divorce can be more stressful than death.

Three out of four married women will become widows. Becoming a widow or widower upon the death of a spouse means facing some of the greatest changes in life, and making new decisions. After sharing life with someone else, a widow must learn to live alone without being lonely. She must handle the daily problems on her own, without sharing the burden with a spouse. She must adapt to changes in relationships with other people and her own image of herself.

Let me begin with the last one. It took me several months after the sudden death of my husband to realize that I had not lost my husband. I knew where he was. But I had lost myself and my identity as the wife of Walter Trobisch. It was an uncomfortable discovery, and I can't think of anything good about it — except that it is a challenge to growth. I also had to accept the fact that there was no one on this earth anymore for whom I was number one.

In the years since Walter's death, I have observed others who face this great blow in their lives. I agree with Daphne du Maurier when she writes:

> No matter how brave a face she puts upon her status, the widow is still a lonely figure, belonging nowhere, resembling in some indefinable manner the colored races in a world dominated by whites.

> The attitude of the non-widowed is kindly, hearty, a little overcheerful in the attempt to show the bereaved that nothing is different, just as the liberal white will shake his black brother by the hand, smiling broadly, to emphasize equality. But neither is deceived and both are embarrassed. There can even be a kind of apartheid. The widowed and the non-widowed withdraw to their separate worlds, and there is no communion between the two.

> The old saying that time heals all wounds, is only true if there is no hidden infection, if the wound has been cleansed. To be bitter, to lament and be filled with remorse (why didn't I . . . ?) can make the wound fester, renewing the sharp knife-like pain and causing the wound to bleed anew.[6]

"You've got to stop the bleeding points," a woman doctor told me a year after Walter's death when I shared in tears the great pain I still felt. She listened and helped me do just that, so that healthy tissue could grow again in my heart rather than scar tissue.

"What is your secret?" I asked an eighty-year-old widow in my neighborhood.

"Do, and go," she answered. "I can still drive and I never miss the chance to attend special events. A woman always needs something to look forward to."

I have learned to face only one day at a time. Each day is a challenge, a test of courage. Pain comes in waves. Accept it. Let the deep pain hurt. Do not suppress it or attempt to hide grief from yourself. It takes time for the newly deaf, blind or handicapped to develop an extra sense to balance their disability. Even so, the bereaved will find new strength and new vision, born of the very pain and loneliness which seem, at first, impossible to master.

Lynn Caine has given us these practical suggestions which she calls her "Survival Kit."

Survival Kit for Loneliness

1. Breathe deeply.

2. Realize you are not the only one.

3. Let your body help you.

4. Pray and meditate.

5. Eat—you need energy and strength.

She says of her own experience:

I was not hungry, but I made tea, scrambled an egg, peeled an orange—and ate. I felt much better. When the body is drained of energy, one loses control . . . The worse one feels, the less one eats. And the less one eats, the worse one feels. When the body needs food and

does not get it, there is a chemical reaction that inten-
sifies depression and loneliness. That is why so many
elderly people are often depressed. It is the result of bad
eating habits.[7]

Remarriage

Lynn says this about second marriages:

> They are far more complicated than first mar-
> riages. One brings more emotional baggage, more life
> experience – good and bad – habits . . . It is not just
> the two of you – love-dazzled and carefree – the second
> time around. There are your children, your family, your
> in-laws, his family, his in-laws . . . All these people
> play a part in your new union – whether or not you like
> it – because they are a part of your life. And that means
> that the number of adjustments to be made in a second
> marriage verges on the staggering.[8]

In my book, *Learning to Walk Alone,* I wrote about
remarriage. "The temptation to try to replace a beloved
partner is strongest in the first year after experiencing
loss," but that is too soon. The wounds have not healed yet.
"Certainly remarriage in God's time and with His choice is
a great testimony to the institution of marriage. But what
God desires, He must also inspire. He gives only the best
to those who leave the choice with Him. It is wrong to push
open a door that God has closed."[9]

Life will never be the same for us again. For me,
marriage was not just another love affair – for those of us
who were married three decades or more, it was at least
half of our existence. We can never give to another partner
what we gave to the partner who is gone. For us, the years
ahead, perhaps ten, twenty, even thirty, may have to be
traveled alone.

My tranquility came as I made peace with my
memories. "What you had, no one can take away from you,

Mother," my oldest son said to me in my early grief. I no longer hear the familiar footstep, nor the voice calling from another room, but there is in the air an atmosphere of love, a loving presence and even merriment when our family gathers together, a time that Walter loved so well.

Finding My Hidden Strength

Today I read Psalm 84, the song of a pilgrim. His eyes are on the goal: Jerusalem. He looks forward to the joy of arriving there. He has to go through the valley of weeping and finds there a place of springs. Verse 7 says: "They go from strength to strength." In my German Bible the translation reads: *"They stride forward with ever-increasing strength, because they see God in Zion."*

For those of us who have gone through the experience of losing our life partner, there is a glimpse through the keyhole into heaven. We have faced one of the worse things that could happen to us, and we have survived. There is a joyful serenity and a holy hilarity in our hearts which helps us keep things in perspective—to see the little things as little and the big things as big. Nothing can rock our boats quite as violently ever again.

Tapping Your Hidden Strength

1. Review the author's suggestions for restoring love to a marriage. What will you do this week to begin applying these ideas to your marriage?

2. What are the pressing emotional needs of a person who has recently gone through a broken relationship or engagement? A divorce? The death of a spouse?

3. Reflect on losses you have endured in your past. How did God sustain you? What has He taught you about life and about His love for you?

4. In what ways is God leading you to minister to an acquaintance who has recently suffered the loss of a love through death, divorce or broken relationship?

CHAPTER 10

Parenting Older Children

Eight principles for strong relationships

As parents, we like to wear our children like a string of pearls around our neck and show them off, don't we? Perhaps some of us just want to be quietly thankful. What do we do, though, when the string breaks and our children deliberately disobey? One of the rules of child-rearing is to respect and trust them. Is it possible to continue trusting even while learning mistrust or the "erosion of trust," as Dr. John White calls it?

Parental Pain

To love a child in this way means that we keep our eyes wide open and are willing to endure the pain — trust within mistrust. We stand waiting and watching, like the father of the prodigal son.

In a *National Geographic* magazine, Dr. Alex Shigo, known as the "tree doctor" in Durham, New Hampshire, said that a tree wears the scars of every battle it has fought. The tree cannot heal itself so it has to wall off the wounds. To inhibit the growth of microorganisms, the tree loads cells around its wound with a sealing substance that acts as a great protective wall. When a giant forest tree is felled, a knowing eye at the planing mill can inspect the dissection and read the story of all the tree's wars. He can discern when the protective bark was broken by a snapped-off limb or an axeman's blade, when the bacteria and fungi invaded the exposed wood and caused decay, when lightning struck, or a woodpecker drilled, or a hungry deer gnawed, or a fire raced by. The scars are all there.

What a story of life! Possibly my deepest scar was inflicted when I received a letter from one of my children saying, "Let me go my way. I know your standpoint on this issue . . . " My first reaction was one of great pain, as if a knife went to the center of my heart.

Then I heard the word from Psalm 118:17: "I will not die but live, and will proclaim what the LORD has done."

The last book that my husband and I read together was *Parents in Pain,* written by Dr. John White (who was mentioned at the beginning of this chapter), a Christian psychiatrist and father of five. Walter was reading it aloud to me and we were in the final chapters at the time of his death.

Dr. White wrote:

> Parenting is a cruel battle between tenderness and contempt. In the months and years of darkness we learned lessons we could never have learned in the light. God is a parent who is willing to share the secrets of all parenting. In Him we found joy and peace.[1]

Now, as a widowed, single parent, I went back to the book, for I was "a parent in pain." I felt understood and comforted by Dr. White's message.

Not Really Ours

We like to pretend that we own our children and are

totally responsible for them and for how they turn out. I've learned, however, that my children are only guests in the family, a temporary trust from God. They are "mine" only in the sense that God counts on me to love them, pray for them, discipline them and train them. The question is not, How can I rear my children successfully? but, How can I become a good mother?

Dr. White reminds us,

> God gave each of us a free will that we use. The problem arises when we find that our children have one too and are using it . . . Our child is *much more* than an extension of ourselves. You cannot ever control another human being, even if that human being is your own child. God has placed your child's ultimate destiny within your child's own hands. This thought was like a rope to hold on to in the dark, a way to grope forward when I could not see ahead.[2]

The idea that parents are responsible for their children's failures is false. Parents are not responsible for their children's successes, either. The problem is your child's, not yours. Until he wants with all his heart to deal with it, until he himself cries out for help — to Christ, to you — nothing will ever take place. It is important that he knows you are on his side, that you are his ally, the ally with the deepest desires and longings for his welfare.

"When the mind is ready, the teacher will come," is an old saying from the Talmud. We can preach and teach until we are blue in the face, but if the mind and spirit are not ready to receive, our words will be in vain.

My child may do something that causes me anguish, but I cannot force an admission of guilt out of him. I can only encourage it and give him the opportunity. At the same time, I need not be intimidated by my child's anger or bitterness. These arise from fear and guilt. I cannot help my child by worrying myself sick over him. I must live with the problem. I must "remain under the pain. That's where the gain is."

One of the hardest things in the world to know is when to press an issue with our children and when to let it ride. We must be prepared for anything, though. When our expectations are disappointed, that can surprise us into an explosion we will regret later.

Children in Pain

Perhaps one of the greatest battles we have to fight for our children is teaching them patience. They feel they need instant gratification when they experience sudden anxiety. Even those who use drugs can't wait a minute for the effect. "Crack" takes only 22 seconds. We need to help young people learn to cope with acute disappointment. If we can get them to wait just overnight to express their negative reaction, by morning the whole picture may have changed for them.

Young people need room to recover from pain, and they need a way to cope with suffering. One escape method they apply is to eat something sweet. It tastes good and is gratifying for the moment, but usually leads to an even lower emotional state. Teenagers like to wallow in depression according to Dr. Sol Gordon, a New York psychiatrist who specializes in the problems of teenagers. Gordon believes that only 5 percent of such depressions have pathologic origins. Because it is so exhausting to be depressed, young people often respond by being mean.

Dr. Gordon told us at a recent workshop that the best thing we can do for such teenagers is to teach them something new. For instance, low self-esteem often goes with not knowing how to read – the child feels stupid.You can't unblock one block with another block. In a program in New York, several illiterate youth were first taught how to swim, and then they were taught how to read.

Dr. Gordon advises teenagers: "If you have an interest, someone will be interested in you. For two weeks don't say anything negative about yourself."

"We need a reservoir of good events to draw from — good memories," he told us. "A sure-fire way to create a happy memory would be to say, 'You have a beautiful smile.'"

After the workshop, I copied Dr. Gordon's essential truths into my journal. They gave me insight regarding my own experience with young people, and maybe they will help you:

- Never touch a kid except in love.
- Develop a relationship.
- You have to save one person. "If you can save one person, it's as though you've saved the world" *(Talmud)*.
- Be helpful to someone else who's more vulnerable than you. Do this without any anticipation of return.
- Be like the father or mother you would like to have had.
- Recognize that all meaningful relationships involve risk.
- Use humor to reduce anxiety. Good humor comes from good human condition.
- Realize that *now* is the only time there is.

We have to make teenagers feel that we are treating them as adults, but many times, we really have to treat them as little children. We have to meet their little-children needs. Dr. Ross Campbell explains this in *How to Really Love Your Teenager:*

> Teenagers are children in transition. They are not young adults. Their needs, including their emotional needs, are those of children. One of the most common mistakes parents, teachers and others make regarding

adolescents is to consider them junior adults. Many people in authority over teenagers overlook their childlike needs for feeling love and acceptance, for being taken care of, and for knowing that someone really cares for them.[3]

The Sexual Battle

Another battle we must help our teenagers fight is the one for sexual wholeness. "If you're not controversial, you have nothing to say; you're boring," Dr. Gordon told Walter and me. We were controversial. When Walter's book, *I Loved a Girl*,[4] came out, it literally made ripples around the world. I often meet Christian leaders who tell me that their lives were changed because of it. We took a clear stand on the subject of chastity—abstinence from sexual relations before marriage—years ago. We believed that God has put up this fence in order to protect our youth, not to confine them.

Promiscuity represents only a faint possibility of love. Desperately lonely people who want someone to touch them often seek that closeness in sex, but such a superficial experience gives no satisfaction. For a girl, the first experience of sexual intercourse is usually grim. According to Dr. Gordon, who has talked with many girls, no girl has an orgasm the first time she has sex.

This kind of inappropriate sex is never an acceptable basis for marriage. Nor is sex within marriage enough to keep marriage going. Dr. Gordon also says, "Marriage fails when it's not an intellectual, rational decision. It's built on trust, humor and communication, with sex and household duties coming in 9 and 10 on the list. Marriage is hard work every inch of the way." He concludes, "It's a good idea to marry the right person in the first place. Give your children the message: 'I don't want you to have sex.' Talking to them *does* inhibit inappropriate behavior. Get your children to plan and to think through their plans."

Communicating

Communication with your children is vital, and it enables you to carry out the discipline (which is not punishment but teaching) and training the children must have.

In order to communicate properly one must know how to listen accurately and sympathetically and have a determination to understand. But most of us are more eager to speak than to listen. Our desire is to be understood rather than to understand. James 1:19 (KJV) says: "Be swift to hear, slow to speak." Both we and our children must be free to express and exchange not only everyday information, but also our own feelings, attitudes and views.

Using one of these responses can help us:

"Could you say that again? I didn't understand exactly"; or, "I can see what you mean"; or, "You must feel bad about that."

Here are some good rules for communication — between spouses as well as between parents and children:

- Pay more attention to understanding than to being understood, to listening than to speaking.
- Learn to recognize when you're upset.
- Express your feelings clearly and simply, not accusingly.
- If disagreement remains, realize that it's all right to agree to differ. Never pretend there is agreement when there is not, and do not insist on resolving every argument.

Parental Unity

The welfare of children rests more on parental unity than on any child-rearing expertise the parents may have. I'm sure you have heard this, too: "The best way to love your child is to love the mother"; or, "The best way to love your child is to love the father." I experienced the comfort that comes from this approach at an early age with my own parents. My brothers and I were disputing one day which one of us might be our father's favorite. We were going to put him to the test when he came home from a trip that day and see which child he greeted first—that one would certainly be his favorite. I shall never forget the moment when he got out of his old car, looked at us all with love, and then said, "Your mother is first." When my parents embraced in front of us, I had a warm feeling of security. Because they belonged together, their love sheltered us all and kept us safe. That was true *Geborgenheit*. Parents can get away with many mistakes if their children see them as a solid, loving alliance.

My favorite poem in this regard was written by Joseph Bayly in his little book, *Psalms of My Life:*

A Psalm of Love

Thank You for children
brought into being
because we loved.
God of love
keep us loving
so that they
may grow up whole
in love's overflow.[5]

Single Parenting

It is important for children to see unity between their parents, but what about when you are a single parent? I know what it means to be a single mother and to have to carry the burden of being both mother and father, just as my own mother did before me. I had to learn this after Walter's early death.

Currently one in every five households is managed by a single person. In many places, the ratio is one in three or four. Before they are eighteen, 45 percent of all children born now will live with only one of their parents part of the time.

Pastor John Yates of Falls Church, Virginia, established a Family Life Action Group in his congregation. As a result he wrote a handbook for those who wish to begin such a group. Knowing Pastor and Mrs. Yates personally has been a great gain in my life and I am thankful to recommend their program. In his book, *For the Life of the Family,* Pastor Yates gives the following advice:

Being a single parent is one of the most difficult tasks imaginable. Therefore, since you are attempting such an overwhelming job, you need the support and encouragement of others. But there is more to it than that. Your child needs the friendship of these [other] parents also. If you are the mother of a young boy, the men in your group can offer him something that you cannot— the friendship and example of a Christian man. God has promised to be a "father to the fatherless" (Psalm 68:5), and one of the most wonderful ways He will do it is through the men in the Body of Christ around you . . .

Many conscientious single parents are tempted to give themselves fully to only two commitments—their children, and their vocation that enables them to financially *support* their children . . . If you have opened your heart in faith to Christ, then you are *not* a single person. You are wedded to the Lord in a way that means He shares in your life completely. You do not "parent alone" if He is in your life . . .

You face great tests as a single parent. You will be tempted to despair, to run away, to feel sorry for yourself, and to hate yourself. You will doubt God's love, you will be overcome by a sense of personal inadequacy, and you will be tempted to hate your former mate (if you are divorced) . . .

Single parents can succeed with the help of God. Your task is not impossible. It is worth remembering that some of history's greatest men and women grew up in a single-parent home and were raised by courageous, dedicated parents. One example from the Bible is that of Joseph, the great-grandson of Abraham . . . If ever a young child experienced trauma, it was this little boy Joseph. For months his family was involved in a headlong flight across the wilderness. [His father Jacob was] running away from an enraged father-in-law, running back to a possible still enraged twin brother, Esau. They had no safe place to call home, and during this time Joseph's beautiful mother died. Throughout this period, his ten older half-brothers shunned him, wanting nothing to do with this boy who was his father's favorite . . . Circumstances were against Joseph ever amounting to anything other than an insecure, frightened, bullied and, at times, spoiled young man. Yet, by God's grace and through his relationship with his father Jacob, Joseph became a great man of God . . .

Jacob was far from perfect. But he loved his son, Joseph, and that love expressed itself in three clear ways: by devotion, discipline and direction. You cast direction in your child's life by what you are. If you truly desire to follow the Lord, then your child will see it . . . Sometimes, as a single parent, you may feel uncomfortable, alone or inadequate. Don't cave in to these feelings. Acknowledge them and then ask God to give you anew and afresh, the sense of assurance, that even though you don't have a mate, you have Him, and for now, He and His people around you are all you need.[6]

I can testify to the truth of these words, having experienced some of my growing up years without an earthly father. God is a father to the fatherless, and I have learned that He is also a helper to the helpless. It was a great release for me as a single mother struggling to keep my perspective in parenting when a kind friend said, "Ingrid, your child is not your problem, but God's problem." At that moment I realized that God was, indeed a father to my child and a helper to me.

Becoming a mother — going through the act of

giving birth—is not something you do only once for each child. I have observed in my own children that they go through seven-year cycles in their physical and emotional development; they are literally re-born every seven years. There is always one, it seems, who is in a special time of need and new growth. As a mother, I must stand by and be ready to bear each child again and again in prayer and love. I could not do it alone, for then I would be "almost to the ground" as it says in the old spiritual. I have learned that I must let each of my children be "God's problem."

Relinquishment

We need to learn the secret of relinquishment, of letting go and allowing our children to be God's. Dr. and Mrs. John White say:

To relinquish your children does not mean to abandon them—but to give them back to God, and in so doing to take your hands off them. Relinquishment means to forsake the right to be proud.

Let your boast be in God's goodness to them and to you in all He has taught you through them and in the privilege He gave you of watching over them. What greater privilege could there be than to be entrusted with care for a new life for God?

Relinquishment also means to give up the right to uninterrupted enjoyment of your children. We can poison enjoyment unless we are prepared to relinquish our right to it. Having joy in my children may be my privilege, but it is never my right. To relinquish your right to their attitude means to give up your right to uninterrupted tranquility. It almost means to give up your right to respectability.

The Whites conclude:

We must give our children the dignity of letting them face the real consequences of their actions. To do so will be painful. Beware of selling your heart in bitterness. The test of godly maturity will be to carry out the sentence combining tenderness with firmness which Samuel says in his farewell address to the people of Israel: "Far be it from me to sin against the Lord by failing to pray for you; and I will go on teaching you the way that is good and right."[7]

Hannah's Blessing

Hannah's prayer for a child caused her to pour out her heart to the Lord. The first chapter of 1 Samuel tells the story:

When Eli, the high priest, accused Hannah of being drunk, she said, "Not so, my lord, I am a woman who is deeply troubled . . . I have not been drinking wine or beer . . . I have been praying here out of my great anguish and grief."

"Go in peace," Eli answered her, "and may the God of Israel grant you what you asked of him."

She conceived and had a son and called him Samuel, because, she said, "I asked the LORD for him."

Hannah then gave her child back to the Lord. She relinquished, much as Dr. White says we must, her right to possess, to enjoy, to be proud before her rival, even her right to control Samuel's development and to be repaid for all her tears.

Her son went on to change the history of Israel. The making and molding of such a character is the work of God Himself.

The wonderful song of praise which Hannah sang in 1 Samuel 2 has always lifted my own heart. "There is no rock like our God [Geborgenheit] . . . The bows of the warriors are broken, but those who stumbled are armed with *strength*." Later on in that chapter we read that every year, Hannah visited her son and took him a little robe which she had made. She sewed her mother love right into it, knowing that it was her way of covering him. She was blessed by the priest who said to her husband Elkanah, "May the LORD give you children . . . to take the place of the one she prayed for and gave to the LORD . . . And the LORD was gracious to Hannah; she conceived and gave birth to three sons and two daughters."

Letting Go of Our Children

I have often repeated a recipe I heard for raising children: "Have them; love them; let them go."

But when it came time for me to let go of my last child, when my youngest left home for good, I discovered how hard it was.

Over the years, women have said to me, "Mrs. Trobisch, my nest is empty. What shall I do?"

I used to reply nonchalantly, "Fill it up quick."

But it wasn't that simple. If I added up the ages of all my children, I had been a mother for almost 150 years. There were the weddings—five in eleven years—when I had to "let go" of each one of my children in a public event. I had heard that the lowest point is a woman's life is when she launches her last child. Was my heart big enough to do as Anne Lindbergh declared in her poem "Even"?

Him that I love, I wish to be
Free—
Even from me.[8]

My heart was experiencing the spiritual truth which Elizabeth O'Connor shared in her book, *Cry Pain, Cry Hope.* In the chapter entitled, "Letting Go," she wrote:

Moses cried out to Pharaoh, as life cries out to us, "Let my people go." How do we do that? I know of no other way except to give one's blessing and to mean it

. . . Jacob needs the blessing of the father if he is to leave the home of his childhood, and we need the blessing of each other to be set free . . . [9]

A mother in Australia, who has teenagers and young adults, wrote to me:

> *In a book of meditations on the passion of our Lord, I read this sentence: "Through Jesus' battle in Gethsemane, He proved that the mightier the fruit of our ministry, the more sacrificial the way will be and the less meaningful our path will appear." As my family grows older, I see that one does not "let go" easily. One cannot but help suffering with them, as they experience life in these truly difficult and dangerous times. We want to hold them close and protect them, but that is not God's way— I see that now. He needs us to allow Him to deal as He will with our children. If they are to serve Him in this hurting world, then they need to have experienced some of the hurt and pain themselves.*

The most important relinquishment I had to learn was to allow my children to face their own pain. They must drive their own vehicle.

Prayer

A long time ago Walter and I realized that every young person needs help. But we knew that we would not always be on hand when our own needed it. So each time we were privileged to help some young person make a life decision, we prayed that our own children would receive the help they needed from the right person at the right time.

Herman Petit, a great prayer warrior, says that we need to pray in terms of that seven-year cycle of growth. Our children are like little trees which we plant carefully, enriching and watering the soil. Even for a fruit tree, it often takes seven years before we get those first fruits. God calls us to be faithful servants in tending the tree. Sometimes the tree needs to be bound to a pole in order for it to grow up straight as well as to be protected from the winds that might snap it off. Then there comes a time, just as in the adolescence of a child, when the tree is ready for the pole and cord to be removed. Otherwise the tree cannot grow independently strong. This is one of the most crucial times in the lives of our children for the power of our hidden strength to come into play.

I know of no other power as great as prayer. It brings heavenly forces to operate in the home and in the lives of those we love.

One of my cousins has five children just the same ages as my own. When her children were very young, she suffered the tragic loss of her husband when he was electrocuted while trying to rescue the family's pet kitten. My cousin wrote to me recently, saying,

> One of my daughters lives constantly in harm's way. And I remember the times when my other children were growing up and making dangerous choices. I decided, "This can't be God's will. There must be something I should do to stop it," instead of waiting quietly for God's will to become clear. But I know now that I must pray for my own faith first, that I can say and truly mean, "God's will be done," before I can pray for my own children.

There is a strong promise in the book of Isaiah which I have claimed for my own family:

All your sons [that means daughters, too] will be taught by the LORD,
and great will be your children's peace (Isaiah 54:13).

Tapping Your Hidden Strength

1. Do you agree or disagree with the following statements, and why? "The idea that parents are responsible for their children's failures is false. Parents are not responsible for their children's successes, either."

2. Rate your communication level with each of your children on a scale of 1 to 10. Then, review the author's suggestions for better communication. Which suggestions will be most helpful to you during the next week? How will they be helpful?

3. Do you and your spouse present a united front to your children? What four things can you and your spouse do to assure your children that you are "number one" to your spouse and that he or she is "number one" to you?

4. How does your personal relationship with God help you in the challenges you face with your children?

CHAPTER 11

Releasing Couple Power

*How one plus one equals
more than two*

I don't remember who said it to me, but the Lord confirmed it: "Learn to stand on your own two feet." After Walter's death, I kept looking over my shoulder for someone to take over his ministry. I wanted to be involved, but I didn't want to take the full responsibility. I wanted to lean on friends, on my children and children-in-love (in-laws), or on Christian leaders. When I sensed that God was trying to get my attention with the gentle nudges of His Spirit, I kept hoping that He would look beyond me. I wanted God to choose someone in the next generation—someone who loved to structure, to plan, to be creative, to lead and to initiate. I felt much more comfortable in the role of nourishing, of taking care of the passengers in the boat, but I certainly didn't want to be involved in steering the course the boat would take.

Letting Go of Our Mate

It took a cycle of seven years after Walter's death before I could say yes to God's call for me to make the vision happen. I had to let my husband go and realize that God was telling me to learn to walk alone. Memories, good as they were, could not sustain me for the stiff climbing ahead.

"Walter died. You didn't. Keep on," a friend put it tersely. I didn't want to listen to her. I was convinced my life, too, was nearly over.

Before my beloved grandmother died, she called me to her bedside and blessed me in my call to go to Africa. Two months before Walter died, I had to lead a marriage seminar without him in Indonesia, and he blessed me to that end. We saw God at work launching a new movement of "releasing couple power" in that country. Now — in my widowhood — it was time for a new step. I was encouraged by a letter from a Canadian friend:

> May the Lord continue to bless you abundantly in your pain . . . this time of letting go. The Lord asked for similar surrender of your mother when your father died, as He also did of His own mother. Continue on your way rejoicing and be assured that your witness to us all is supported by the love and prayers of the worldwide community to whom you have both given yourselves unreservedly. "I am going there to prepare a place for you . . . You know the way" [John 14:2,4].

Letting go means that we will be lonely. We think of those feelings of loneliness which we had as a child or young adult because we felt rejected. But facing this pain of letting my life mate go was a part of standing on my own two feet, something God was trying to teach me. Meister Eckhart, a Christian mystic, put it best when he said, "Our letting go is in order that God might be God in us."

I told about this letting go in *Learning to Walk Alone*:

> In order to survive and grow out of my subjectivity, I followed certain physical laws of health: a balanced diet, adequate fluid intake, daily exercise and

enough rest. I enjoyed going swimming, because for a few minutes I could "swim away" from all that was burdening me. At times I experienced clear guidance about my next step.

This happened one day when I went swimming with Betty, who was soon to marry my oldest son. Daniel had asked whether he might have his father's wedding ring. As Betty and I were standing in the corner of the pool between laps, I took off my ring and gave it to her. I *was* married to Walter Trobisch and what I have had will not be taken away. But now death has parted us. I must let go in order to go forward.[1]

The psalmist said, "God is our refuge and strength, an ever present help in trouble" (Psalm 46:1). *Refuge* is another word for *Geborgenheit*. God Himself promises to be our place of safety and security. What more could we ask?

A New Ministry

"Each one of us needs an idea for which he is ready to live and to die," Soren Kierkegaard once said. I asked myself, *What am I ready to live and die for? Now that I have let go, it's as though Jesus touched me, just like he touched the woman who was bent over. I can stand up straight again. What does He want me to do during the next period of my life?* According to Gail Sheehy's *Passages*, I'm just beginning the seven years of "middle adulthood"—this could be the best seven-year cycle of my life.

Without any hesitation I knew my goal: to be an instrument in helping release couple power. What is "couple power"? It's the multiplied power of two whole people joined as man and wife. Two people together can do more than two separately, especially when they know that as man and woman they have been created in the image of God. Together they mirror His image to the world.

Both our masculine and feminine sides need to be developed if we are to reflect God's image to a broken world. What better way to make couples aware of this than to organize weekend retreats for them? I thought of at least a dozen couples right away who would be interested in this down-to-earth experience. I wanted to call the weekends "Quiet Waters Retreats" — seminars that could be held in different centers throughout the United States. More than six hundred couples had already been trained in Germany in such weekend retreats, using the structure Walter and I had developed, and the effect of their "healthiness" was contagious.

Three Stages of Love

We all go through three stages in our "love" development: the auto-erotic phase (*auto* means self), the homo-erotic phase (*homo* comes from the Greek word which means same) and the hetero-erotic phase (*hetero* means other).

I am convinced that many marriages, and many individuals, are still in the first stage: "I want what I want when I want it." This is a normal level for babies and small children. It's a sickness of our time and it is called "instant gratification."

Others are stuck in the second stage. As we grow up, it is good and healthy that boys have boy friends and girls have girl friends. We need to be able to express our feelings and share what we are thinking with members of the same sex. Only then do we become strong enough to face the opposite sex.

The mature stage of love is the hetero-erotic stage — the love relationship between a whole man and a whole woman. Our German pastor told us what it meant for him to love his wife:

The loving man is not one who is seeking to be loved, but his great happiness is to give love. Then his wife can respond. That which you like to receive, you must give. To win a whole heart means to give a whole life. Marriage, that close relationship to one woman, is a man's training ground. There he is allowed to practice and learn that which gives him authority for all other areas of his life and profession.

So many of the young people today—yes, even Christian young people—think that if they can just meet the right partner, all of their problems will be solved. But the problem solving must be done within the person himself or herself rather than through someone else. Young people need to be challenged to become healthy, whole individuals, accepting both their masculine traits and their feminine traits.

Couple Power

We want to encourage the growth of two whole people, man and woman. Then when they come together we have a third whole. That's couple power. It begins with 300 percent and keeps multiplying as husband and wife allow each other to blossom and grow. If two half-portions, Mr. 50 Percent and Miss 50 Percent, get married, they often cancel each other out and are fortunate if added together they make 25 percent. Time, money, sex—all create problems for them, and they need to find and develop insight and wisdom.

As observed earlier, marriage is hard work. It is not a goal, but a growing. To be effective, a couple needs nurture, a continual feeding on the strength which rises from each person's secure and loving relationship with the Source of all strength.Without this feeding, the marriage will be like a fire which burns brightly for a while, but then since no new logs are added it goes out. An untended fire soon dies and becomes just a pile of ashes.

A wife needs to know from her husband, "You're OK for me." It's easy for her to doubt this when she sees her husband, this all-sufficient man, going forth to his daily work outside the home while she's coping with dishes, diapers and discipline. She wonders, *Does he really need me? Wouldn't he be able to do more for the Kingdom of God if he were not married, if he were a celibate as Jesus was?* A wife's greatest emotional need is "the need to be needed" and to be recognized for her own worth.

"Does your wife work?" someone asked my son-in-law, David.

"She certainly does," he replied, "a lot harder than I do. Katrine is at home with our pre-school children and believes in her calling as a 'people-maker.'"

And what about the man? What is his greatest felt need? I believe that a man can be more easily and deeply wounded in his heart than a woman. Dr. Paul Popenoe, well-known author on parenting and family relationships, says, "Men are hard, but brittle. Women are soft, but tough." Women can flex more; they can cope easier. Suicide rates are higher for men, and more men than women die of heart attacks.

In *All That a Man Can Be,* Walter wrote:

> The role which we men cannot play comfortably is that of being the strong sex. We strain and strain at it and still our performance is not very credible. We may have illusions about ourselves in our early years, but later in our marriages we find that we cannot earn much applause for our efforts. The real woman sees through such pretensions and would like to ask her husband to be just a kind human being and not some sort of super-man.[2]

Dr. R. Affemann, a German author, says,

> To love is a continuing process of facing disil-

lusionment and disappointment in the other one. This task has to be faced anew every day. Only in this way will the relationship of love be close to reality. True happiness is not built on false images, but on truth.[3]

Love sees the other one as he is and accepts him that way. Love means, too, that *I can let myself be seen by my partner as I am, knowing that I will be accepted that way, too.*

Roots of Infidelity

But what does the uncomfortable man do? He defends himself because he's afraid of being hurt. He suffers acutely when he feels threatened, and, suffering, he becomes the man who reacts. His last resort is the unfaithfulness of adultery. Many men who pretend that their strong sexual desires push them to extramarital sexual activity actually are suffering without realizing it because their ambitions and hopes in other realms have been unfulfilled.[4]

The other root of infidelity is the desire for *Geborgenheit,* that wonderful German word we have been adopting which means more than shelter, refuge and security all in one. *Geborgenheit* is the foundation on which marriage stands. It comes from the word *bergen* which means "to rescue; to bring into a safe place." *Burg* is the German word for fortress, stronghold, castle. Therefore, we are talking about the secure place we have been brought to where we have nothing to fear. In a marriage which is alive, each partner feels secure, has no fear, is at rest with the mate; each is convinced that his or her spouse wants only the best for the other one. Does a husband give his wife this *Geborgenheit?* Does a husband find this feeling of shelter when he is with his wife: Where is it lacking? It can be his fault. It can also be her fault. But mostly neither partner is providing it.

The aim of our Quiet Waters Seminars is to help marriage partners find their *Geborgenheit* and share it. Through the teaching, which first brings couples to knowledge, then insight, and finally change of behavior, we want them able to release their couple power. The seminar involves a lot of written dialogue, and those exercises help each individual to get in touch with his own feelings as well as those of his partner. Christ loves us as we are, but He doesn't leave us as we are. We teach our couples this basic relational principle: "You cannot change your partner; you can only change yourself — and the Lord is waiting to help you."

It's been my privilege to know couples who are already changing the face of the globe through their couple power. I think of the twelve couples in Germany who have worked as teams for more than ten years — the ones who have trained the six hundred other couples in their retreat center. A participant said to one of the leading couples, "It's not that you have anything so revolutionary to say, but you say it together — and that's what counts."

The three main roots of couple power are *grace* (forgiveness), *commitment* and *acceptance,* which are found in that private, secret, safe relationship with our loving Father. In biblical times Priscilla and Aquila, the husband and wife mentioned by Paul in 1 Corinthians 16, were releasing their couple power in the church that was in their house, and others were finding their own inner strength because of it. Our goal is to see that happen now, today, and here, in our own country.

Tapping Your Hidden Strength

1. What is "couple power?" Apply the author's definition to your own special relationship. In what ways do you think God wants to use the two of you to accomplish His purpose?

2. The author states, "Marriage is hard work. It is not a goal, but a growing." Do you agree? Why or why not?

3. Name five things a man needs from his wife on a continuing basis, then five things a woman needs from her husband, to keep the flame burning.

4. What are three areas in which your spouse needs regular *Geborgenheit?* Come up with at least one idea for how you can help provide that sense of rest, security and shelter in each area.

CHAPTER 12

Finding the Way Home

*Our place in Christ — and
the gift of inner strength*

When Stephen, my youngest son, was asked to share a tribute about his father in a family letter, he wrote:

> *Father will always remain in my memory as a "traveler." Especially when I was younger, it was one of the hardest things for me to see him and mother leave. But in the moment we were all back together again it seemed as if all the waiting, all the longing and the feeling of being left behind was completely blotted out.*
>
> *I can well remember how he asked me once what would make me happy. I said, "The coming back home."*
>
> *His answer: "How can you come back home if you have not been away from home?"*

Where Home Is

Some of our hidden strength comes from knowing where our home is. Recently I returned from a six-week trip to five European countries, including East Germany. During that time, I seldom spent more than two nights in the same bed. I lived out of my suitcase. For a few weeks, my Bible, my copy of the Moravian Daily Texts with the pictures of my family pasted on its blank pages, my journal and my notebook became my "home." Could I have made it without knowing that after six weeks of such living I would return to my "place" in Springfield, my *Haus Geborgenheit?* I don't know. The day I safely returned, my heart was filled with praise to my heavenly Father for providing me with this home base. I think I felt what the Israelites felt when they went back to Jerusalem after being in exile: "We were like men who dreamed. Our mouths were filled with laughter, our tongues with songs of joy" (Psalm 126:2). If there is such joy when we return to our earthly homes, imagine the joy of our reaching our heavenly home!

Henri Nouwen writes in *Lifesigns,*

> When Jesus says: "Make your home in me as I make mine in you," He offers us an intimate place that we can truly call "home." Home is that place where we do not have to be afraid but can let go of our defenses and be free, free from worries, free from tensions, free from pressures. Home is where we can rest and be healed.[1]

My oldest son Daniel and his wife Betty work with troubled youth in Austria. One day I turned to my son and asked, "What is your goal in your ministry?"

"To show people the way home," was his quiet answer.

My Goals

Recently a good friend remarked, "Ingrid, I get tired when I look at your schedule."

I had to be honest. "Yes, Lil, I get tired, too, but it's worth it."

There is a sense of quiet urgency in all that I do, an inner voice that says, "Do it now." I have learned to enjoy the sacrament of the present moment. I try to "work smarter, not harder." I've also learned that it's not enough to be efficient. I must be effective as well. To do that I need goals which are achievable and which I can visualize.

For example, at a recent Clergy Day in Springfield we talked about life management. The leader invited me to share my goal for this year. Facing that group, I said, "I want to organize and carry out four Quiet Waters Retreats for couples. My purpose is to explode their problems and point them in a new direction—toward their true source of inner strength, a deep, personal, loving relationship with their heavenly Father. I believe this is the best missionary work I can do. If this can rebuild one or two new homes, that in turn can cause people to know the indwelling power of the Holy Spirit, and I will feel that these goals for the year have been reached."

Establishing these four retreats meant getting a leadership team together, finding the right locations, and praying for the participants. "Make three phone calls every day," the group advised. It worked. Each retreat overflowed into the next one. Now we're setting dates for next year. Someone has aptly said, "The longest journey begins with the first step." I love to get people started on their homeward trek.

When I moved to Springfield from the Lichtenberg a few years ago I found a hundred-year-old cabin on my property. The roof was caving in, but the chimney and fireplace were sturdy. The ceiling beams were hand-hewn and still intact. My pioneer cabin stood slightly atilt because a strong tree was growing at one of the corners. I asked a builder friend what he thought about restoring the cabin. His reply was, "Ingrid, give me a match and I'll set fire to it!"

But the next day he came back with practical ideas on how to reconstruct my historic little building and what it would cost. I cashed in my insurance policy to finance it, and my two strong nephews helped with the project. Three months later we had a celebration — a dedication in the "New Life Cabin." I enjoy the simplicity and quietness of it and I am reminded of that verse which became my watchword when I moved here:

> The LORD will guide you always;
>   he will satisfy your needs . . .
>   and will strengthen your frame.
> You will be like a well-watered garden,
>   like a spring whose waters never fail.
> Your people will *rebuild the ancient ruins*
>   and will raise up the age-old foundations;
> you will be called *Repairer of Broken Walls,*
>   *Restorer of Streets with Dwellings.*
>   (Isaiah 58:11,12, italics mine).

"It's all right."

At the time of this writing, I have five little grandsons six and under. When you hear their names you know the vision of their parents: Peter, Andrew, Michael, Charles and James. And I have three granddaughters: Christine, Virginia and Margaret Helen. Margaret Helen is a Down syndrome child and has already been God's messenger to our family. She has taught us the secret of what it means to "let yourself be loved." When I got the news of her birth and told my son Stephen, he said, "It's all right, Mother."

These were the same words of the Shunammite woman whose story is told in 2 Kings 4:8-37. When her beloved son died, she told the prophet, "Everything is all right." It was a word of acceptance and at the same time faith in what God would do in the situation. She was a woman of quiet confidence and persistence, and she had found her inner strength. She was already on her way home. Her faith was honored and the prophet restored her son to life.

The inner strength is described by Paul in Romans 5:5: "God has poured out his love into our hearts by the Holy Spirit, whom he has given us."

In *Winter Grace*, Kathleen Fischer quotes Thomas Merton's description of centering prayer as "finding one's deepest center, awakening the profound depths of our being in the presence of God who is the source of our being and our life."[2] *His description fits hidden strength as well.*

This inner strength comes as a gift, but we have to accept it, unwrap it, and begin to appropriate it. Being in our own place at our regular time, ready for close communication with our Father, gives us a sense of stability and prepares us to receive the gift.

It is helpful to begin by focusing our minds on spiritual breathing. As we exhale, we breathe away all our fears and worries, we confess our sins, and we acknowledge God's forgiveness through Christ's death on the cross. When we inhale, we breathe in the love and life of God, appropriating the fullness and power of His Spirit by faith. We obey God's command to be "filled with the Spirit" (Ephesians 5:18), which actually means to be continually controlled and empowered by the Holy Spirit. When we have claimed the fullness of the Holy Spirit, we can walk in faith and experience the abundant and fruitful life which Christ has promised us.

I have found it helpful to begin my prayer times with words from the psalms, for example:

> Keep me safe, O God,
>> for in you I take *refuge*.
> I said to the LORD, "You are my Lord;
>> apart from you I have no good thing" . . .
> I have set the LORD always before me.
>> Because he is at my right hand,
>> I will not be shaken . . .
>>> my body also will rest secure . . .

> You have made known to me the path of life;
>> you will fill me with joy in your presence,
>> with eternal pleasures at your right hand.
>>> (Psalm 16, italics mine.)

He has promised to lead me beside quiet waters and to restore my soul (Psalm 23).

He promises you the same:

> He *who dwells* in the shelter of the Most High
>> *will rest* in the shadow of the Almighty . . .
> He will cover you with his feathers,
>> and under his wings you will find refuge.
>>> (Psalm 91:1,4).

Only there — in His shelter and refuge — is true *Geborgenheit*. There you will find your source of hidden strength and genuine serenity. And there you can rejoice with the unknown writer of the 15th century when he put it this way:

> Thou shalt know Him when He comes,
>> Not by any din of drums,
>> Nor by the vantage of His airs,
>>> Nor by anything He wears,
>> Neither by His crown,
>>> Nor His gown
> For His presence known shall be,
>> by the *Holy Harmony*
>> that His coming makes in thee.

Tapping Your Hidden Strength

1. Jesus said, "Make your home in me as I make mine in you." What does this mean to you personally? How does one make his home in Jesus?

2. Review the principle of "spiritual breathing" in this chapter. Resolve to keep short accounts with God — by confessing sin whenever His Spirit reveals it to you and by appropriating His forgiveness and cleansing. This is the key to growing intimacy with God.

3. Is Jesus Christ your *Geborgenheit?* Have you placed any other person or thing before Him? Make Him your place of serenity, security and shelter today.

4. Read Isaiah 58:11 aloud and personalize it by substituting "me" and "my" for "you" and "your."

From a
Mother's Heart

Just before the birth of her fifth child, my oldest daughter, Katrine, had four quiet days away from her family. Her youngest son, Charles, almost three, was puzzled by her absence and said to his five-year-old brother James, "I think Mommy died and went to heaven."

Their father, who was listening to the conversation, heard James wisely reply, "No, she's just in Disneyland." (That is where Christine and Virginia, his two big sisters, were spending time with their grandparents.)

Katrine, sequestered in a friend's guest room on the Florida coast, spent those four days writing these meditations for young mothers. She wrote them for the time when her own daughters would be facing the same experiences she was going through. They are from the heart of a mother, and both Katrine and I want to share them with your heart.

Like Paul in the book of Acts, Katrine and her husband, David Stewart, think of themselves as tentmakers. They have served at various posts throughout the world for the U. S. Foreign Service Corps, and are in Pakistan at the time of this writing.

— Ingrid Trobisch

Our Lord does not care so much for the importance
of our works
as for the love with which they are done.
— Teresa of Avila

The waste of life lies in the love we have not given,
the powers we have not used,
the selfish prudence which will risk nothing
and which, shirking pain, misses happiness as well.
— Anonymous

1.

From now on all generations will call me blessed (Luke 1:48).

I cannot think of one incident in the Bible where a woman considered herself deeply unhappy or even curbed because she became pregnant. Among others, Sarah, Rebecca, Hannah, Elizabeth and Mary considered themselves to have been greatly favored by the Lord when given a child to bear. Mary conceived her child under the most difficult of circumstances. She was yet unmarried. Her fiance was likely to reject her. Her town would disapprove of her. Had she lived in our time, many would have advocated an abortion. Yet when the angel appeared to Mary, she did not utter a word of complaint. We all can learn from her example!

Recently, when I was just beginning to show with the pregnancy of our fifth child, a woman came up to me during a Christian meeting. I didn't even know her. She felt an immediate need to pray for me. She asked the Lord to erase all the negative things said about my pregnancy. I was grateful for her prayer. I then pondered the direction of our society if we must pray for such things.

God does show us His favor when He lets us bear a child and thereby become a part of His creation in progress.

Prayer:

We praise You, exalt You, glorify You, because You have given us the gift of life.

Challenge:

Channel your thoughts of bitterness and resentment against insensitive people into a humorous vein. Prepare a few gentle, funny comebacks to meet the sarcasm you may draw. Learn to laugh at even the rudest observations.

Or when someone approaches you with words like, "My, you certainly have your hands full," you can reply with a "soft answer" such as: "Would it not be sad if they were empty?"

2.

Each one of you also must love his wife as he loves himself, and the wife must respect her husband (Ephesians 5:33).

Your husband has to be your ally. You can't pull the family wagon without him. Voice your feelings of frustration, envy, even anger, and talk them over. Try to be constructive. Don't nag. Your husband can only understand you and show his concern for you in a tangible way if you keep explaining to him what is going through your mind. You yourself know how complex your feelings are.

In our times, more so than ever before, both husband and wife are subject to the unending task of communicating with each other. If the marriage partners don't make an absolute priority of taking time out to talk together, other "communications" (and you know which ones I mean) will quickly take over any available space.

The key person to your happiness as a mother is your husband. You can stand frontline battle if he is on your side. When someone asks David whether I work or not, he likes to say, "Katrine works harder than I do." That kind of recognition and acknowledgment from within the ranks gives me strength to stand up against the pressures of the outside world.

Prayer:
Please touch the hearts of unsympathetic husbands.

Challenge:
Take time out to write a love letter to your husband. Thank him for enabling you to be a full-time mother. Do you realize that this is becoming more and more a privilege and a luxury in our society?

3.

Carry each other's burdens (Galatians 6:2).

We hear this command so often. What does it mean to us? How can we put it into action? The closest burden we feel and carry for someone else is probably the burden of our own sick or injured child. We may suffer immensely for an emotional injury inflicted upon our child or husband. Christ knows this and He has again put us mothers into a special privileged position where we may learn firsthand what it means to carry the burden of another.

Resolve that the next time a friend is sick you will not just say over the phone, "I'll pray for you," and then maybe not even do that. First, think of what you would do for your own child if he were sick. Then think again of what you can do for your friend. Our heavenly Father loves us as His very own children. We should, as best we can, try to imitate that kind of love amidst our circle of friends and acquaintances.

Be devoted to one another in brotherly love (Romans 12:10).

Let us not love with words or tongue but with actions and in truth (1 John 3:18).

Prayer:

We thank You for the uncounted opportunities to help carry another's burden.

Challenge:

When a friend (or grandmother?) tells you again, "Let me know if there is any way I can help," take her at her word. Make up a list and put it into her hand. Here are some suggestions:

Help me so I can plan ahead for some time all by myself.

I am looking for some good reading material while nursing the baby, preferably something which you have read and appreciated yourself.

4.

[Love] is not self-seeking (1 Corinthians 13:5).

Sometimes the never-ceasing tasks of motherhood make us feel alone, unhappy, miserable. All mothers at times think they cannot bear the responsibility and the time commitment of raising a young child. And yet, with our innermost being, we know that we cannot and would never run away from that responsibility. "See to it that you complete the work you have received in the Lord" (Colossians 4:17).

At this point, some of us discover a new dimension of guilt. We look into those innocent, demanding, loving eyes and realize that we can never fully give what those pleading eyes are asking for. No, we cannot give ourselves unconditionally to that little soul or for that little soul. Nor can we do it for our husbands. We realize that, when left to our own resources, we often are unable to give the amount that is needed in order to have peace within our homes. We are afraid that our husbands will take us and our tasks around the house for granted.

More acutely than ever before, we become aware of the fact that we cannot love perfectly. Nor do we have to. This quotation might help to remind us of strength and love from another source: "The living Christ still has two hands, one to point the way, and the other held out to help us along."

We should try to let our mother love be a reflection, if but imperfect, of the heavenly Father's love for His children. Others should not know us by our negativeness, bitterness, frustration. Instead, we can radiate compassion, patience, humility and gentleness.

Prayer:

Thank You, Lord, for teaching us a new dimension of love through our children. (See Luke 6:38.)

Challenge:

Read 1 Corinthians 13:4-8a aloud and insert your own name for the word *love*.

5.

*[Be] confident of this, that he who began a good work in you will carry
it on to completion until the day of Christ Jesus* (Philippians 1:6).

People often say, "This is just the way I am! Nothing can
change that"; or "This is just the way things are around here!"
When we resign ourselves to such thoughts, the devil is tempt-
ing us to acknowledge defeat. Then the battle is over. The only
thing in this world which does not change is God. We can alter
our circumstances considerably, especially if we ask God for advice, assistance and strength. And God has the power to change
us according to His own good purpose.

Don't give up when the baby cries for the fifth time in
one hour – or if he cries endlessly. Giving up is defeat. Try to
think what went wrong, what threw you off, or what threw the
baby off. Reorganize your forces. Think of a new approach. Any
good general would do the same when he recognized an un-
desirable situation. Set yourself a different plan of action for the
next day. For instance, change the baby's nap time. Should he
wake early, let him just stay where he is. Put distance between
you and him. Let him cry, if necessary, before you go to him. Dis-
tract yourself by reading a good book. Set a timer.

Guidelines like that do wonders for your peace of mind.
Every step of the way, ask God for wisdom (see James 1:5). He
will carry out His work within us. "I will instruct you and teach
you in the way you should go; I will counsel you and watch over
you" (Psalm 32:8).

Prayer:

Thank You, Lord, for new beginnings.

Challenge:

Analyze your daily schedule. Which parts of it are you
the least happy with? How can you change them? Be creative and
constructive. "Commit your way to the LORD; trust in him and
he will do this" (Psalm 37:5).

6.

Your labor in the Lord is not in vain (1 Corinthians 15:58).

We should not take ourselves too seriously. We all have shortcomings. We should make the valleys of our life as beautiful as possible for we know that we will soon return to the mountaintop. Staring with teary eyes of anger and resentment at these peak experiences will not bring them any closer. Nor will it make our valley any more livable. Only hard work and determination will carry us back on high.

You may feel that your husband finds more fulfillment and acknowledgment in his professional job than you do in your job as a mother. Assess your feeling. Ask yourself, What can be more important, teaching many children how to add or teaching one child about the Savior?

You are like a master artist working at your life's greatest work. You must keep for yourself the vision of your finished masterpiece. Others tend to see only the roughly cut stone which you appear to chisel at in vain. They observe a mass of squealing, dirty, unruly, youthful humanity and rarely find words of encouragement, for they lack your vision. Accept your calling and realize that immediate recognition of your work will be exceedingly sparse.

Prayer:

Lord, cleanse my heart from envy and resentment.

Challenge:

Share your feelings of anger, frustration and envy with your husband. Ask him to reassure you more often. He needs your communication in order to understand you. A baby has the right to be understood without words—an intelligent adult does not. Maybe your husband can help you to think of something special which you can look forward to in the *near* future.

7.

If anyone does not know how to manage his own family, how can he take care of God's church? (1 Timothy 3:5).

C. S. Lewis has said, "One must not assume burdens that God does not lay on us. It is one of the evils of the rapid diffusion of news that the sorrows of *all* the world come to us every morning. I think that each village was meant to feel pity for *its own* sick and poor whom it can help, and I doubt if it is the duty of any private person to fix his mind on ills he cannot help."

We have a great opportunity for outreach right in our homes. Mothers often experience guilt in terms of the small amount of time and money they are able to spend on outsiders. Remind yourself that you are growing, nurturing and producing a crop that may not bring you financial reward, but will later greatly influence the world in which we live. Little outside employment can offer such long-lasting results.

Prayer:

Lord, grant me strength to love and nurture my own family so that they can in turn love and nurture others.

Challenge:

Write down the names of those who live in your home. Think of their specific needs. Decide how you can help them to meet these needs. Set yourself practical goals. You may add to your list those who regularly visit your home and those whom you would like to invite into your home. Keep the list in your Bible. Check periodically on the progress you are making in meeting the needs of those on your list.

P.S. Do not forget to include yourself on the list, somewhere after your family and before your friends. Check periodically also on the progress you are making in meeting your own needs.

8.

In his heart a man plans his course, but the LORD determines his steps (Proverbs 16:9).

Don't set unrealistic goals. Your numerous required tasks and constant interruptions have already fragmented your time into hundreds of little mosaic pieces. There is no reason to crowd your day more by goading yourself to write a letter daily, read one chapter of a book daily, do whatever else daily . . . When we do this, at the end of the day we feel grieved, guilt-stricken and frustrated if we have not achieved our goals. We are angry at our children, our husband and the world as a whole.

God gives us twenty-four hours each day. We can then logically conclude that there will be enough time in every day for those things which God deems important. Our need for personal achievement can confound our willingness to accept and fulfill His priorities. Christ ministered in a small geographical area and personally reached relatively few people. Yet He rested contentedly, even though aware of the multitudes outside Palestine that He was not helping, because He knew He was fulfilling His Father's priorities.

Prayer:

Please give me the strength and discipline to do one thing at a time and to do it well.

Challenge:

Make a list of all the things you would like to have a little time for *each day*. Rank them in order of priority. For example, "quiet time" comes at the top of my list.

9.

It seems that I don't have time to think anymore. I'm running empty. There are no sparks in my mind. My spirit wants to fly, but where to? Why is my life not more colorful, dashing, romantic? Marriage can be such a dampener. Children all the more so.

I have just finished reading a beautiful historical novel. It makes me feel so frustrated not to be able to share in my own life the excitement, adventure and romance of the main characters.

Then a wonderful thought strikes me: *Day after day, my husband and I are living out our own life's novel. Our story does not end with the dashing conquest. To the contrary, that is where it begins! With God's help and much hard work we are trying to turn the "happily ever after" myth into a reality. We see many couples who don't find fulfillment in their home life and seek it elsewhere, in activities ranging from overactive church work to video addiction . . .*

Yes, the Lord does lead me beside quiet waters (Psalm 23:2). When I seek His comfort, He comforts me — as He did just now while I was writing this.

Prayer:

From the bottom of my heart I plead with You, Lord. Restore my soul. Give me rest.

Challenge:

If at all possible, try to put your children to bed early and keep your evenings free from housework. Take time out. Come up for air.

10.

Serve one another in love (Galatians 5:13).

Love, if we want to follow Christ's example in our lives, has little to do with self-fulfillment. To the contrary, the love of Christ has much more to do with service and sacrifice. Father used to say, "Marriage is not just moonlight and roses. It is also dishes, diapers and even dirty socks with holes in them."

Sometimes we only love our partner the way we think he deserves to be loved. In our human way, we treat him exactly how he deserves to be treated. God does not love us only as much as we deserve to be loved. Mother Teresa encourages us to love the way Christ did. She says we are to love until it hurts. Mothers, love the way Christ did! Love to the point of sacrifice, not just to the point of your own happiness. When we do not actively seek happiness we receive it abundantly as a reward from others.

God is the source of all love, wisdom and understanding. He not only loves us for what we are, but also never fails to love us for what we can become.

Prayer:

As the demands on us grow, help us, Lord, to increase our capacity for love.

Challenge:

Take a piece of clean blank notepaper. With your husband in mind, print at the top of it, "Why do I miss you when you are gone?" Think of at least three answers and write them down. Tape the paper inside your husband's closet door, with your photograph if you have one.

P.S. The next time your husband has to go on a trip by himself, slip a surprise into his suitcase. How wonderful a personal love message can be in an empty hotel room.

11.

*You will not have to fight this battle. Take up your positions; stand
firm and see the deliverance the LORD will give you*
(2 Chronicles 20:17).

We need to focus on long-term goals. This conflicts with
the modern demand for instant gratification. When we do think
about our long-term goals, we realize that they often are not very
tangible. Nobody can guarantee us that our children will turn out
beautifully, no matter how much effort we put into them.

Nothing on earth exceeds the value of the young ones
whom God has entrusted to us mothers. We are making people!
There is no higher calling. Regardless of how self-fulfilling paid
employment may be, no job compares in importance with that of
being a mother. We are raising and shaping the future generation. We lose our self-esteem when society tries to convince us
that we are replaceable. They tell us that essentially anybody can
do our work, nearly causing us to give up our efforts, which we
often believe are unappreciated anyway. The theory that our husbands can completely replace us in our motherly responsibilities
can be deadly poison to a marital relationship. It is simply un-
true, and therefore will not bear up under the test of time.

Take up your positions! Stand firm! We have got to dare
to swim against the stream. The battle is not ours, but God's (2
Chronicles 20:15). A German poet put it this way: "Dare to be
sand in the machinery of this world."

Prayer:

Help us not to be afraid or discouraged, Lord, as we stand
up for our convictions.

Challenge:

If you don't have a close friend nearby, boldly pray for
one. God loves you. He will not give you a stone instead of a friend
(Matthew 7:9). You need to be able to encourage each other in
your independent mothering. Maybe you can help each other in
some very practical ways, too, such as baby-sitting, car-pooling,
shopping and the like.

12.

Practice hospitality (Romans 12:13).

As more and more women join the work force, fewer and fewer homes remain intact, self-reliant units. If meals are eaten at home at all, family members often do not eat them together. If nobody spent much time preparing them anyway, there is little loss. Since people increasingly are seeking their emotional support outside the home, if we try to keep our own hearthfires burning, we can warm some of those who have lost theirs. I have experienced the gratitude of those "needy" people and found it worth all my efforts. We can turn our very own homes into mission fields.

Prayer:

Our God and Maker, please pour Your lovingkindness into broken homes and help to mend them.

Challenge:

Plan and prepare a very special dinner party for one evening after the children are down. Include invitations, placecards, candles, flowers, three or more courses (elegant but simple) and whatever else you like, such as some special entertainment. The number of guests is up to you. If you're not used to this kind of thing, start with two. In terms of atmosphere, your home with its very own personal touches can certainly outrank any restaurant. Don't worry too much about the food. Where there is interesting company and conversation people are often not even aware of what they are eating. You may be surprised at what a dinner party like this can do for your self-esteem.

13.

With joy you will draw water from the wells of salvation (Isaiah 12:3).

Cinderella is one of my favorite fairy-tale characters. She has such a beautiful and gentle spirit. No amount of suffering and hard work seems able to crush it. She does not realize during her hardship that her suffering will soon cease, nor that a loving fairy godmother is watching over her. Suddenly one day her rags literally turn into riches. Had she howled and rebelled against her lot, the end of the story would never have been the same.

Do you see parallels? We like the story. We like the way Cinderella handles the burden of her sad fate. Yet many of us refuse to learn from her. We even know that a loving God is watching us, which is more than Cinderella knew. But because we cannot see, we often do not believe.

"With joy you will draw water from the wells of salvation." That is just one promise from our heavenly Prince, and He has given us many more. He has even told us that He is with us wherever we go. He says that we need never be afraid! How much more comfort that is than what Cinderella had. We can strive cheerfully to follow her example because we know the happy ending in store for us!

Prayer:

Thank You for our earthly princes.

Challenge:

Start a diary of projects, ideas and innovations that come to mind when you read the Bible. Write down things you'd like to do. Write down even the silliest things. Keep your notepad at hand and jot down thoughts when you're reading, working or listening to a speech. Take it with you when you travel or visit relatives. Sometimes the greatest thoughts come when you're away from your daily routine. Winston Churchill used to say, "A change is as good as a rest."

Then refer to your idea notebook whenever you feel you're running out of steam.

14.

And be thankful (Colossians 3:15).

As mothers we are not discovering new dimensions of just love – we are also discovering new dimensions of gratitude. How privileged we are! Sometimes I feel that God is putting us mothers through a special fast-track curriculum in His school of life and holiness.

You will never again have the same attitude toward time that you had before you gave birth. I consider quiet moments during the day so precious now that I have learned to bow my knees in reverence when those moments arise and to thank God for His valuable gift of time.

Another of our problems is that we often feel unappreciated and taken for granted by others. And yet, here is a list of luxuries which I completely took for granted myself before our home was peopled by children: The luxury of a long, private bath. The luxury of making order around me which I knew would remain. The luxury of spending time on my hair and personal appearance without feeling that I was wasting precious moments. The luxury of uninterrupted Bible study and prayer. The luxury of waking up and getting up at my own time. The luxury of walking through stores without watching little people and feeling the pressure of time schedules. The luxury of leaving things anywhere I chose without worrying that little hands might hide them, break them, tear them, eat them?! The luxury of dreams, ideas, rambling thoughts – and no one to disturb them.

Prayer:

Thank You for teaching me to thank You, Lord, and not to take anything that comes out of Your hands for granted.

Challenge:

Make a list of at least three things you are grateful for. Tape it on the refrigerator. Whenever you have a chance, sing it out loud for the whole family to hear.

15.

He lifted me out of the slimy pit (Psalm 40:2).

How often I forget that He can lift me out. It seems that I wallow in my pit, in my depression . . . and I want to say, "No, Lord, don't lift me out. I won't even let You try. You might want me to start to sing [see Psalm 40:3] and I can't do that. I'm too tired. Baby Charles is sick. I ate too much. My period is due any moment. Nobody truly loves me or understands me. Nothing is going the way I want it to go. I'm doing the same things over and over again. My hair is unwashed and uncombed. I haven't even gotten properly dresed yet. No, Lord, You don't want to lift me out. You don't even want to look at me right now."

We shouldn't put God and the whole rest of the world (husbands included) on hold while we're feeling depressed and sorry for ourselves. Depression is often caused by disobedience in little things, such as undisciplined eating and sleeping habits. In our hearts we know we are not pleasing our Maker, our family or our friends. Yet this causes us to wallow self-righteously in our pit of defensive self-pity. Instead of pulling ourselves together and confronting ourselves in a mirror and through the eyes of others, we find all sorts of "valid excuses" for withdrawing, and we prefer to live in an unhappy vacuum. The psalmist David knew what I am talking about. He was in that very same situation many times and talked often and openly about it. His plea was, "Turn to me and be gracious to me, for I am lonely and afflicted" (Psalm 25:16). Isn't this often the case for young mothers? Isolation leads to depression . . .

The first "easy" step out of a depression is to start focusing away from yourself. Realize there are other people even more depressed than you. You may be able to help them better than anyone else because you know exactly how they feel. Do let go of yourself. Let God lift you.

Prayer:
Make Your comforting and uplifting strength known to

those who are depressed, Lord. "You need not cry very loud: He is nearer to us than we think" (Brother Lawrence).

Challenge:

Analyze what causes you to become depressed. Write it down. Next to each cause of depression write a solution. Some solutions may come to you faster than you think. *Fatigue — Rest*, for example. The difficult part is to put your solutions into action. Good luck!

A Final Word

Offer your bodies as living sacrifices, holy and pleasing to God
(Romans 12:1).

As mothers of young children we must learn the greatest sacrifice of all. We must learn to give our time and our life to others. We cannot give it in one great, earthshaking gesture, however. How much easier that would be! That which we are able to give, our time and our life, we must give in thousands of little pieces so that others may be nurtured steadfastly.

Could we possibly learn to collect and accept the scattered fragments of our time and shape them into one glorious mosaic? With God's help, maybe we can.

Prayer:

God, please help me to piece together my "shattered" life. Help me to find joy in gathering and assembling the thousands of pieces. Inspire me and grant me a vision of what the whole mosaic "picture" will look like one day.

Challenge:

Sit down and take time out to read for one hour. Count your interruptions. Try to turn each one into a beautiful creative thought. For example: The baby needs to be changed. Think of how you not only want your child to be clean in body, but you also want him to be pure in heart and spirit. Remember how so often your own outer appearance is a reflection of your inner condition. Imagine each interruption to be part of something larger and greater.

Try your hand at writing a psalm, patterned after those in the Bible. [Use the format below if you like.] Keep it as personal as a diary. When finished, retype the words on a 3 x 5 card and tape the card in your Bible as Psalm 151.

O LORD, You know me inside out — when I feel _____ or think _____. Even then I know You will understand. My future is laid before You.

You know my concerns about _____ and how I worry about _____. But I know I can trust You to guide me.

I give thanks to You, O LORD, even though _____ and even when _____, because I know You are in control, no matter what. You are the stronghold of my life.

I shall not fear _____ or concern myself with _____. For You will hold me, protect me, and comfort me all the days of my life.

We praise You, we exalt You, we glorify You . . .
because You have given us the gift of life.

Reference Notes

Author's Preface
1. Ingrid Trobisch, *On Our Way Rejoicing* (Wheaton, IL: Tyndale House, 1986).
2. Ingrid Trobisch, *The Joy of Being a Woman . . . and What a Man Can Do* (San Francisco: Harper & Row, 1975).
3. Ingrid Trobisch, *Learning to Walk alone* (Ann Arbor, MI: Servant Books, 1985).

Chapter 1
1. Joyce Kilmer, "Trees," *The Best Loved Poems of the American People* (Garden City, NY: Doubleday & Co., 1936), p. 561.

Chapter 2
1. Walter Trobisch, *All That a Man Can Be* (Downers Grove, IL: InterVarsity Press, 1983).
2. Leanne Payne, *Crisis in Masculinity* (Westchester, IL: Crossway Books, 1985), p. 141.
3. Ibid., p. 13.

Chapter 3
1. Ann Spangler, ed., *Bright Legacy* (Ann Arbor, MI: Servant Books, 1983).
2. Quoted in *My Journey Homeward,* by Walter Trobisch (Ann Arbor, MI: Servant Books, 1986), pp. 19-21.

Chapter 4
1. Dave Veerman, "Did I Marry the Wrong Person?" *Practical Christianity* (Wheaton, IL: Tyndale House, 1987), n.p.

Chapter 5
1. Nanci and Randy Alcorn, *Women Under Stress* (Portland, OR: Multnomah Press, 1986), p. 90.
2. Walter Trobisch, *Martin Luther's Quiet Time* (Downers Grove, IL: InterVarsity Press, 1975), pp. 14-19.
3. Alcorn, *Women,* p. 25.
4. Ibid., p. 9.
5. Ibid., p. 38-39.
6. Quoted in "Our Forgotten Day of Rest," *Today's Christian Woman* (July/August 1987), pp. 31-33.
7. Karen Mains, "Our Forgotten Day of Rest," p. 32.

Chapter 6
1. Robert Johnson, *We: Understanding the Psychology of Romantic Love* (San Francisco and New York: Harper & Row, 1983), n.p.
2. Walter Trobisch, *I Married You* (San Francisco: Harper & Row, 1971), pp. 75-77. Adapted.
3. See Ingrid Trobisch, *The Joy of Being a Woman* (San Francisco: Harper & Row, 1975), chapter II, "The Wife's Joy in Sexual Response," pp. 6-32.
4. Ibid., p. 24.
5. Mike Mason, *The Mystery of Marriage* (Portland, OR: Multnomah Press, 1985), p. 45.

Chapter 7
1. See Ingrid Trobisch, *The Joy of Being a Woman* (San Francisco: Harper & Row, 1975), chapter III, "Living in Harmony With the Cycle and Fertility," pp. 33-64.

Chapter 8
1. Sharon Donohue, "Sorting Out What Matters," An Interview with Becky Pippert, *Partnership* (July-August 1987), pp. 15-21.

Chapter 9
1. Walter Trobisch, *Love Is a Feeling to be Learned* (Downers Grove, IL: InterVarsity Press, 1971), p. 14.
2. Marion Hilliard, *A Woman Doctor Looks at Love and Life* (New York: Doubleday & Co., 1957), n.p.
3. Robin Norwood, *Women Who Love Too Much* (New York: St. Martin's Press, 1985), n.p.
4. Jean Vanier, *Man and Woman He Made Them* (Mahwah, NJ: Paulist Press, 1985), p. 112.
5. Walter Trobisch, *I Married You* (San Francisco: Harper & Row, 1971), p. 23.
6. Daphne du Maurier, *The Rebecca Notebook* (Garden City, NY: Doubleday & Co., 1980), p. 276.
7. Lynn Caine, *Lifelines* (Garden City, NY: Doubleday & Co., 1978), n.p.
8. Ibid.
9. Ingrid Trobisch, *Learning to Walk Alone* (Ann Arbor, MI: Servant Books, 1985), pp. 89,94.

Chapter 10
1. John White, *Parents in Pain* (Downers Grove, IL: InterVarsity Press, 1979), n.p.
2. Ibid., pp. 56-58.
3. Ross Campbell, *How to Really Love Your Teenager* (Wheaton, IL: Victor Books, 1981), n.p.
4. Walter Trobisch, *I Loved a Girl* (San Francisco: Harper & Row, 1965).
5. Joseph Bayly, *Psalms of My Life* (Wheaton, IL: Tyndale House, 1969), p. 12. Used by permission.
6. John Yates II, *For the Life of the Family* (Wilton, CT: Morehouse-Barlow, 1986), pp. 4-9.
7. White, *Parents,* pp. 167-69.
8. Anne Morrow Lindbergh, "Even," *The Unicorn and Other Poems* (New York: Random House, Pantheon Books, 1972), p. 14.
9. Elizabeth O'Conner, *Cry Pain, Cry Hope* (Waco, TX: Word Books, 1987), p. 50.

Chapter 11
1. Ingrid Trobisch, *Learning to Walk Alone* (Ann Arbor, MI: Servant Books, 1985), pp. 46-47.
2. Walter Trobisch, *All That a Man Can Be* (Downers Grove, IL: InterVarsity, 1983), pp. 35-36.
3. R. Affemann, *Sexuality and Sex Education in the Modern World* (Gerd Mohn Verlag, 1979), n.p. Translated from German.
4. Trobisch, *All That a Man,* p. 54.

Chapter 12
1. Henri Nouwen, *Lifesigns* (Garden City, NY: Doubleday & Co., 1986), p. 27.
2. Quoted by Kathleen R. Fischer, *Winter Grace* (Mahwah, NJ: Paulist Press, 1985), p. 24.